ben webster

Jeroen de Valk

Ben Webster
his life and music

Berkeley Hills Books
Berkeley California

published by:
Berkeley Hills Books, PO Box 9877, Berkeley CA 94709
www.berkeleyhills.com

distributed by:
Publishers Group West

library of congress cataloging-in-publication data

Valk, Jeroen de, 1958–
[In a mellow tone. English]
Ben Webster : his life and music / Jeroen de Valk.
p. cm.
Translation of: In a mellow tone : het levensverhaal van Ben Webster.
"American and completely updated edition"—Pref.
Includes index.
ISBN 1-893163-17-2 (alk. paper)
1. Webster, Ben. 2. Jazz musicians—United States—Biography. I. Title.
ML419.W39 V3513 2000
788.7'165'092—dc21

00-012014

photographs:
p. 16 courtesy of Joyce Cockrell
pp. 35, 51, 55, 59, 104, 172 Duncan Schiedt Collection
pp. 94, 116 © Lee Tanner / The Jazz Image
pp. 9, 11, 15, 146, 155, 182, 191 courtesy of the author
p. 250 © Cecco Maino

table of contents

preface

Writing this book was a time-consuming undertaking. Ben Webster (1909–1973) has been dead for more than twenty-five years, and has not been honored with a biography until now. Fortunately, friends, musicians, jazz experts, and even some remaining family members were willing to supply me with information.

I would like to thank Rob Agerbeek, Harold Ashby, Joost Aukema, Whitney Balliett, Tom Beetz, Egbert de Bloeme, Henk Bouwer, Jopie Byas, †Arnett Cobb, Joyce Cockrell, Pierre Courbois, Yvon Delmarche, Maarten Derksen, Fred Dubiez, John Engels, Jan Evensmo, H. Fluitman, Iwan Fresart, Sheila Gogl, Rein de Graaff, Eric Ineke, Bertil Jacobi, the Darmstadt Jazz Institute, John Jeremy, George Kaatee, Johan van der Keuken, Peter Krijnen, †Ruud Kuyper, Herman te Loo, Jaap Lüdeke, Hans Montijn, Dan Morgenstern, the Nationaal Jazz Archief, Harley Robinson, Irv Rochlin, †Jimmy Rowles, †Michiel de Ruyter, Han Schulte, †Han Sinot, Cees Slinger, Joop Spuyman, Jesper Thilo, Wim de Valk, Han Veelders, †Dolf Verspoor, Bert Vuijsje, Henny ter Welle, Henrik Wolsgaard Iversen, and Joe Zawinul.

Thanks to my translator Laura Jennings-Blijleven, and publisher Robert Dobbin, who gave me a chance to publish an American and completely updated edition of the book. Publication has been made possible with financial support from the Foundation for the Production and Translation of Dutch Literature; I thank them very warmly as well.

Jeroen de Valk
Amersfoort, The Netherlands
August 2000

chronology

1909 Born Benjamin Francis Webster in Kansas City, Missouri, on March 27, the son of Mayme Barker and Walter Webster. His parents divorce the same year. Raised mostly by his great-aunt, Agnes Johnson.

1917 Starts playing the piano (mostly self-taught) and takes violin lessons for a brief time.

1927 Gets his first professional jobs as a musician. Finishes Western University and goes to Wilberforce University in Ohio for two years.

1929 Works as a piano player in Kansas City. Discovers the alto saxophone and learns to play it in Billy Young's family band, alongside Lester Young. After six months switches to the tenor.

1931 Makes his first recordings with Blanche Calloway.

1933 His father Walter Webster dies in a hospital, at the age of (about) 67 years.

1934 Starts becoming a 'name' horn man, playing in Fletcher Henderson's band where he replaces his idol, Coleman Hawkins. Later in the thirties, tours with Cab Calloway and Teddy Wilson, and records with Billie Holiday.

1940 Joins Duke Ellington's orchestra.

1941 Marries Eudora Williams; they divorce within a few years.

1942 His buddy in Ellington's band, bass player Jimmie Blanton, dies.

1943 Leaves Ellington and works with his own groups in New York.

1948 Returns to Ellington; leaves in the summer of 1949.

1949 Starts living again with his mother and great-aunt in Kansas City.

1951 Moves with them to Los Angeles.

1952 Does his first studio session under the supervision of producer and impresario Norman Granz. In the fifties, for Granz's labels, he records his best work ever. Also tours with Jazz At The Philharmonic. Until 1964, lives and works periodically in (or around) New York.

1957 Granz stops organizing concerts in the USA.

1960 Granz sells his record label Verve.

early '60s Works less and less in New York and Los Angeles, until he is virtually out of work; has an alcohol problem and asks too much money.

1963 His mother and grand-aunt, both in their 90s, die in Los Angeles.

1964 Goes to Europe for an engagement in Ronnie Scott's club (London), and remains in Europe for the rest of his life.

1966 Moves to Amsterdam, where he lives with his landlady, Mrs. Hartlooper.

1969 A couple of months after an enormous party celebrating his 60th birthday, moves to Copenhagen. There he is taken care of by Birgit Nordtorp.

early '70s Heavy drinking once again limits the number of his concerts and recording sessions.

1973 Dies on September 20, in the Lucas Hospital in Amsterdam at the age of 64. Two weeks earlier he had suffered a severe stroke after a concert in Holland. Cremated in Copenhagen, where his ashes are buried.

the brute and the beautiful

Ben Webster ranks among the seven greatest jazz tenor saxophonists, along with Coleman Hawkins, John Coltrane, Lester Young, Dexter Gordon, Stan Getz, and Sonny Rollins. Compared with the other six he wasn't a revolutionary, and it took him a relatively long time to come into his own artistically; he didn't become a presence in the musical world until he was almost 30 years old. After that, it took him another ten years to find his definitive personal style. Yet he belongs in this group because he possessed a distinctive, immediately recognizable way of playing. In the average and slow tempos—where he was most at home—his timing was relaxed, and he produced a warm, sensual sound that he manipulated in many different ways. His trademark was the sound of his breath that he would blend with the notes. Sometimes there was hardly any tone left in the lower register—virtually all you'd hear was breath. At such moments, it was like he was whispering something in his sweetheart's ear.

Although he possessed a raw, tearing timbre that he'd

produce for faster pieces, he was at his best when playing ballads. He often played them in the same manner, but really gave his all at each performance. Under the right circumstances, he continued to play with impressive devotion and authority until the very end of his life.

Ben Webster was a heavyset man, about 5'10". He had a very broad chest, an even bigger stomach, and skinny legs. In the last decade of his life his weight exceeded two hundred pounds, and he started walking with a cane because his legs could barely support his large torso. His skin color was a light brown. He had lost most of his hair by the time he turned forty. He cultivated a thin moustache, and sported some impressive bags under his eyes. On the back of his head he often wore a hat that was a little too small—which enhanced (by contrast) his physical size.

He called his saxophone, the antique Selmer he bought used in 1938, “Ol' Betsy”—nobody knew exactly why. When he died on September 20, 1973, in the Lucas Hospital in Amsterdam, the instrument went to the painter Steven Kwint. Steven was his best friend, and on his deathbed Webster said to him, “Steff, you take care of Ol' Betsy. Don't let nobody play her.”

After the cremation, Kwint's girlfriend and wife-to-be Rens Sevinga opened the saxophone case. It contained not only the saxophone, but also a toothbrush covered in black stains, a comb that had the same black sheen, and a rosary. When she found the toothbrush and comb, she suddenly realized he must have dyed his hair. How else was it possible that his hair, the little that he had of it in his final years, was entirely black, with not a gray strand to be found? Rens remembered he would always put down a handkerchief before lying down on their sofa or sitting down in a chair, to prevent his hair leaving a stain. He might even have used shoe polish. Even though he had grown overweight, he had retained some of his vanity after all.

And the rosary? Webster had a religious upbringing. He liked playing the tough guy, but when he realized his end was drawing near, his religious sentiment returned. Rens Kwint said, "He loved to talk about his good times with Duke Ellington. Musician anecdotes. But when the two of us were alone, he talked about the women who had raised him. He used to be like a big child at those times; he talked about them in such a naive and sincere way. Neither of us was affiliated with a church. 'God is within yourself,' those are the kinds of things he used to say."

Webster lived in Amsterdam from 1966 through 1969. Although he moved to Copenhagen after that, he remained in contact with his Amsterdam friends. "He was surrounded by a sizable circle of friends. Whenever he came over from Denmark, he'd call us all up. Before we knew it, five or six of us would be gathered around his hotel bed with a case of beer, while he was calling the States in his underpants. He needed a lot of company and attention."

⨳

As a young man, Webster had been nicknamed "The

Brute." His large build, expensive clothing, the cocky look in his eyes, and the way he wore his hat on the back of his head, often got him accused of having started fights even when he was only a passer-by. Without fail, policeman would ask him for identification. He had large scars on one of his arms, probably the result of a fight. When a friend once asked him about it, all he would say was, "Glass is dangerous."

In 1936, he pushed a woman out of a window in a moment of blind rage. She survived the fall, but the incident didn't enhance his reputation. He saved at least two people's lives, however: Lester Young, Lester's brother Lee, and probably one other person—an unknown woman he saved from drowning. He never talked about his good deeds; they probably didn't fit with the image he worked so hard to maintain. It wasn't until he moved to Europe that much of his bravado fell away.

He was very attached to his mother and the great-aunt who had raised him. His great-aunt, whose father was an escaped slave, mothered him until shortly before her death at nearly one hundred years of age. Whenever he wasn't staying in New York or on the road, he would usually live with them, until a few years before his emigration to Europe in 1964. "I was very lucky as a child," he would later say. "If I wanted a bicycle, my mother would buy it for me. If I wanted skates, my mother would buy that for me. I think she bought about five bicycles for me."[1]

He was so spoiled that he could get extremely upset when things didn't go his way. These two women were among the few people who could handle him at such moments; Duke Ellington and Benny Carter, two musicians he had the greatest respect for, were two more. The contrasts in his temperament were reinforced by the contrast between the order and refinement he knew from home, and the raw life of the musician he met with in the outside world.

Ben grew up among women, who had taught him better manners and a more polite manner of speaking than those of the other kids in the neighborhood. As a child, kids called him a sissy. No wonder he invested so much energy in his tough guy image later on. Saxophonist and composer Ernie Wilkins dedicated a piece to him, "The Brute and the Beautiful." Wilkins: "He was the Dr. Jekyll and Mr. Hyde of the tenor saxophone."[2]

Tough guy or not, he continued to need women around to mother him. In Amsterdam this was his landlady, Mrs. Hartlooper, who always urged him to finish what was on his plate, and told him not to drink too much. In Copenhagen, he met Birgit Nordtorp, a young nurse. During the last few years of his life, Birgit tried to protect him from himself, as far as that was possible. According to Rens Kwint, "Ben would always find people who'd take care of him. In spite of his appearance and all his whims, there was something childlike about him, which somehow made you want to help him. Whenever he came over for dinner, he really enjoyed himself. He let us pamper him completely. And we'd always have ice cream for dessert—he insisted on it."

According to Dolf Verspoor, another acquaintance, "Ben

was someone who made friends everywhere. Everyone had warm feelings for him, and he himself radiated warmth as well. I don't know anyone else who could put so much feeling into a ballad. He gave these ballads a dimension they hadn't possessed before—because they were initially fashionable tunes, songs out of musicals, without any artistic pretenses. Ben turned them into poetry."

notes

1 From the movie *Big Ben,* by Johan van der Keuken (1967).
2 From the movie *The Brute and the Beautiful,* by John Jeremy (1989).

kansas city

Ben's great-great-grandmother was a woman from the west-African country of Guinea; her name could no longer be traced. In the early nineteenth century, she was taken to the United States in one of the large slave transports. She ended up working for a family in Kentucky. One of the family members—supposedly the head of the household, a Tom Lincoln by name—fathered a son by her. This son fled slavery at a young age. He settled in Liberty, Missouri, and took the name of Missourian Sallé. "Sallé" he copied from a Frenchman he had befriended on the road; "Missourian," of course, referred to his home state.

Among his descendants, the story still goes that the man who got his mother pregnant was president Abraham Lincoln's father. It is true that Abraham Lincoln was also born in Kentucky at the beginning of the nineteenth century, and that, in his only remaining picture, Missourian Sallé shows a distinct likeness to his alleged half brother. That is the only evidence for the alleged connection, however (besides the name).

In Liberty, Missourian Sallé got married to woman their children called "Ma Sallé." They had four daughters. Agnes (b. 1864), probably their youngest child, went on to play an important role in the family. Her husband, Ben Johnson, was an unexceptional man whom she outlived by several decades. Agnes' sister Alice married a Mr. Barker. He fathered five children and died shortly afterward, probably of tuberculosis. Alice then remarried, to a Mr. George Ruff; they had no children. It's remarkable how well Alice Ruff's children have done for themselves, especially considering that she was the daughter of an escaped slave and grew up in poverty. Almost all of them went to college: Mayme became a kindergarten teacher and Lymer a chiropractor. Blanche and Delcina studied domestic science in college.

Although the family enjoyed some financial prosperity, Alice and her new husband had a difficult time keeping the family together. One of them, a boy who went by the curious name of Oner Bell, ran away from home when he was just a boy. During their teenage years, Mayme and Blanche were raised by their aunt Agnes Johnson because Alice didn't have enough time and money to take care of all her children.

Mayme Barker (b. 1872) must have been very unlucky in love. Her upbringing was probably partly to blame: Aunt Agnes took perfectly good care of her, but enforced strict puritanical principles. Mayme was 35 or 36, and still lived with her aunt Agnes, when she married a man some six years her senior: Walter Webster. She had met Walter when she was in Chicago, probably for summer

opposite: Ben's great-grandfather

MISSOURIAN SALLÉ — *Great Grandfather*

school. The couple got married a year later, in June 1908. They followed the tradition of marrying in the bride's hometown but, after the wedding, Walter brought her to live in his apartment in Chicago.

The decision to marry Walter was the biggest mistake of her life. A family member visited the couple in September of that year, and found Mayme in a terrible state: she was suffering from malnutrition, and Walter, a coarse, heavyset alcoholic, abused her physically.

Aunt Agnes decided to intervene. Because Walter refused to let Mayme go, Agnes Johnson personally traveled to Chicago around January 1909 to rescue Mayme. This must have been quite a task for Aunt Agnes; compared to Walter, she was just a polite, delicate woman. She was, however, reputed to be energetic and resolute.

The heavily pregnant Mayme moved in with her aunt again in Kansas City, Missouri. On 2441 Highland Avenue, in a house that has since been demolished, her child was born on March 27, 1909. They called him Benjamin Francis, Ben for short. Mayme wasn't officially divorced at the time of his birth, so he got his father's last name, even though Walter was no longer in the picture at all. Ben was just a baby when he moved to 1222 Woodland Avenue with Mayme and Agnes Johnson. This is where he spent his youth.

Soon after Ben's birth, Mayme returned to her profession of kindergarten teacher. Most of the literature wrongly reports that Ben was raised by his grandmother. The confusion is understandable, as Ben often referred

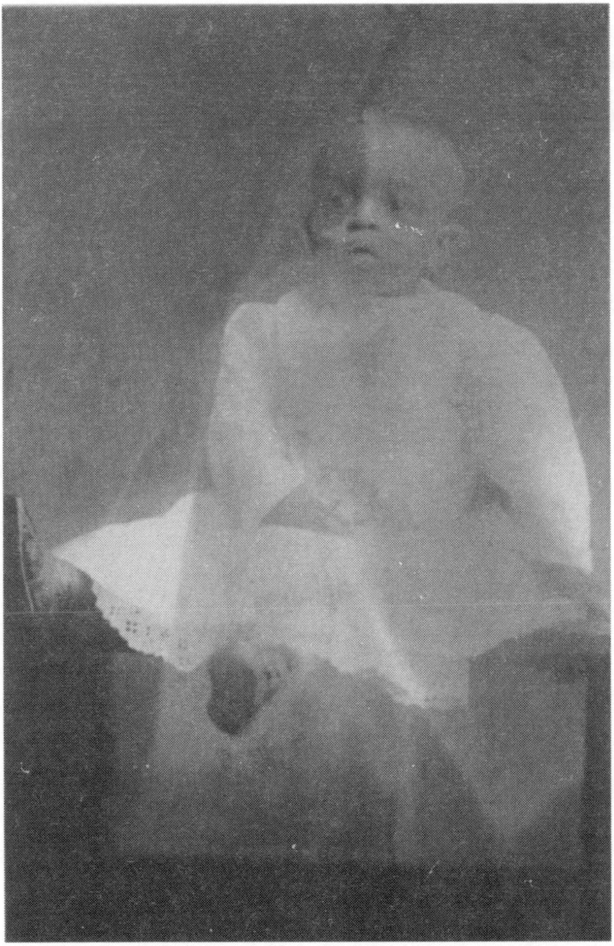

Ben as a baby, approximately six months old: Kansas City, 1909

to his great-aunt as "my grandma." Aunt Agnes, who never had any children of her own, was getting on in years: she was 45 when she took on the care of Benjamin Francis. Mayme and Ben ended up living with her for almost the rest of their lives, and in the thirties, aunt Agnes also took in Harley Robinson, the thirteen-year-old son of Mayme's sickly sister Blanche. Harley lived with her until he went into military service five years later.

※

Most of the above information was provided to me by Ben's cousin Harley Robinson (b. 1919), and his second cousin Joyce Cockrell (b. 1897) who in 2000 reached the venerable age of 103. Cockrell, who was a bridesmaid at Mayme and Walter's wedding, also spent time in the household that Aunt Agnes ruled with an iron fist. She and her first husband stayed there for a few years during the twenties. After Ben Webster's death on September 20, 1973, Cockrell wrote a long letter to Ben's close friend in Amsterdam, Steven Kwint. I quote it here in full:

> September 22nd, 1973
> 4825 S. San Pedro St.
>
> Dear Mr. Steve Kwint—
>
> My name is Joyce Cockrell, and I am one of the only two living relatives of Benjamin on his mother's side. His mother's maiden name was Mayme Barker, and I was her flower girl at her wedding with Walter Webster. Mrs. Webster was a very credited kindergarten teacher and very puritanical in matters of conduct and morals. She was adopted by an Aunt (Mrs Agnes Johnson) who

raised & educated her. Benjamin was borned in the family home at 1222 Woodland Ave, Kansas City Mo, March 27, 1909, where his mother resided with her after separating from his father. Mrs Johnson was a highly political & influential figure in K.C. Mo and yielded the same kind of influence in her home with Mayme & Benjamin. After Benjamin was borned, Mayme resumed teaching again, so Aunt & Benjamin were together most of the time, and believe it or not she indulged Benjamin & downright spoiled him. He had his way about most everything and they both loved one another very much. He called her Mom and all through her life, she came first and this is why he had no family life of his own.

At an early age at the insistence of both Mayme & Mom, Benjamin was given violin lessons. He took lessons for about 5 years, where he learned the fundamentals of the instrument and read notes. This in turn enabled him to play the many instruments he played during his life time. When his many friends began to refer to him as a sissy because of the violin, one day he broke it up on my piano. In his home, there were two pianos, his mother's & mine. At this time my husband & I were living with them. My piano was a Vosc [Vox], with a concert pitch & easy action (I being a musician myself) & he preferred banging on mine. This is where he started picking out tunes & learned to play the piano.

He graduated from Public School, June 10th 1921 with an A & B average. Graduated from Sumner High School K.C. Kansas & then from Western University in Quenemo [?] Kansas June 2nd 1927, also was awarded the Major Letters for positions in football of guard & tackle on Varsity squad. During this time he was very naive in the problems of the outside world, because he had been protected & disciplined. He was sent to Wilberforce University in Ohio, and stayed two years and then came back to Kansas City Mo. He picked up playing piano with his own small five piece group at the Jazz Land and other cabarets, especially at 12th and Vine. He left K.C. with Clarence Loux [?] to Topeka Kansas—through Arizona & then Amarillo Texas—joined Jean Carr's band, from there to Albuquerque New Mexico, where he joined Lester Young's father who taught him trombone & tenor saxophone. He came back to K.C. with Jater [Jap] Allen's band where he stayed about 2 years. He left and went to New York & joined Blanche Calloway's band, from there to her brother Cab Calloway's, then from Cab Calloway to Fletcher Henderson's band. Also Willie Bryant Band and then to Duke Ellington band and stayed 2 [actually, three-and-a-half] years. After he left Duke, he went out on his own doing recordings, special guest for many top bands, night clubs and theatre. He did many Jazz [at the Philharmonic] tours. This was his life in the States, you will have to pick it up from here.

I hope I have been helpful and I thank you for being his friend and being interested.

Sincerely—Mrs Joyce Cockrell.

⁂

Harley Robinson informed me that Agnes Johnson was reputed to be a dedicated fighter for equal rights for blacks as well as women. She led anti-racist action committees, and was involved in the suffrage movement. She was also one of the founders of the Allen Chapel, a Methodist church in Kansas City that all

Mayme Barker, Ben Webster's mother, in front of her apartment in Los Angeles, 1953.

Ben's second cousin Joyce Cockrell with her fifth and final husband, Dennis. Los Angeles, 1955.

family members were expected to attend on a regular basis.

Aunt Agnes and Mayme instilled in Ben a few values they had picked up from the white middle class. Until the end of his life, Ben was of the opinion that a saxophone was a nice instrument, but a violin was really something "higher" (which may help explain his later partiality for 'strings' albums.) He considered the profession of jazz musician no more than a trade; in his eyes, it had little to do with art. In the sixties, in Copenhagen, an eighteen-year-old once came up to him and asked him whether he should go into "the profession." The boy played the bass, and was prodigiously talented. Still, Webster tried to dissuade him: "You're young, you've had a good education, you got all these opportunities... Do you really want to turn into a tramp like me?"[1] Luckily, Niels-Henning Ørsted Pedersen—for that's who it was—ignored his advice.

Ben really looked up to Hilton Jefferson, an alto saxophonist who had nevertheless remained a gentleman. "He's so good with a knife and fork. He can clean off a drumstick better with a knife and fork than you ever could with your teeth. And fish? With knife and fork—never, ever with his fingers."[2]

These women seldom raised their voices, and surrounded him with an atmosphere of strict order and routine. In the fifties, when their son had already played with Duke Ellington and had become world-famous, the balance of power within the household didn't change at all. Pianist Jimmy Rowles said, "He called his mother

Mayme and his grandmother [*sic*] Mom. And Mrs. Johnson was boss in that household. She wanted him to behave right. She was strict, but not bossy. I thought she was a striking woman. His manners were impeccable at home—I don't think they had any idea about his wild behavior outside.

"We'd always go play golf together when we both lived in L.A. But when we were just about to leave, his grandmother always said, 'Benjamin Francis, you haven't cleaned up the yard yet and you have to mow the lawn. Jimmy, you're gonna have to wait.' And I'd listen to an Art Tatum tape that had been playing all this time, while he was doing his chores. And we weren't allowed to leave until he was finished."[3]

※

Ben's father, Walter Webster, was employed on one of the Pullman trains. At the time, that was one of the best jobs a black man could find. Pullman employees had a special status. They received a lot of tips, and rumor went that women would throw themselves at them so as not to be alone at night.

What's also important is that they traveled throughout the United States, and therefore got a chance to pass news along. There already were two large black newspapers in those days—*The Amsterdam News* and *The Chicago Defender*—but if a black man in the South was caught reading either one he ran the risk of getting beat up. Blacks were not encouraged to know what was going on in the world.

Webster met his father on at least one occasion: in Chicago, around 1930. He had gotten hold of his father's address, and wanted to pay him an unannounced visit. Ben found Walter Webster in the company of an uncle—one of his father's brothers—and became aware that, for some reason or other, his presence was not appreciated.

Walter and his brother nervously drank one shot after another. Were they waiting for something? They made up some excuse to try to get him out the door, but Ben didn't want to leave right away. After a while the truth emerged. The doorbell rang, and two prostitutes stepped into the room, laughing and joking. Webster junior laughed his head off, and then saw it best to withdraw. This story later became part of his repertoire of anecdotes.

Shortly before his death, Ben told his Danish friend Henrik Wolsgaard Iversen that his father had been a large, heavy man with Indian blood. He had black hair down to his shoulders. According to Ben, the Indian blood was the reason Walter Webster drank so much.

Walter Webster died in a hospital, lonely and unmarried, in 1933. The death certificate states that he had been working as a "waiter" for the railway until a few months before his death. His date of birth was unknown, his age estimated to be 67. Webster senior had been suffering from a kidney inflammation, and two days before his death, he also contracted blood poisoning.

When he was a child, Ben could not accept the fact that he didn't have a father, according to his second cousin Joyce. "He always wanted to know where his father was.

He kept coming back to Mayme and saying, 'Where is Walter, where is my dad.' And she would reply, 'Well, I don't know.' She never wanted to go into detail about it, tell him what happened. Ben had a very hard time not having a man in his life, not a single one."[4]

※

As Joyce's letter indicates, Benjamin showed a lot of interest in the piano. Joyce lived just a few houses down at first, and he often went over to her house. Because he disturbed her so often when she was trying to study, she decided to give him a few lessons in order to give his enthusiasm some direction. This is how he came to learn the basics of piano playing, without his mother's or great-aunt's knowledge.

Benjamin enjoyed playing radio songs by ear. Whenever he was fooling around on the piano at home, Mayme and Mom noticed how quickly he was progressing. By the time he was about eight years old they decided he was musically gifted, and began giving him the violin lessons. Although this period was important for his subsequent development—he learned to read music, for one thing—Webster himself used to recall it with bitterness.

"I hated that violin. My mother wanted me to be a little lord with a neat collar, taking violin lessons. My friends would call me: 'Sissy with the violin, sissy with the violin.' Practice, practice. Tears all over my face. But when she left the house to teach school, I was on that piano!"[5]

By this time, Joyce had gotten married, and she and her husband David Lewis moved into the large family home with Aunt Agnes. Ben was about twelve years old when one day he got so fed up with the violin that he smashed it on her piano.

Pete Johnson, the well-known boogie-woogie pianist, lived across the street from the family home. Ben recalled how "Pete Johnson learned me how to play the blues, and then I ruined poor Joyce's piano."[6] Other than some informal lessons from Johnson and Joyce, he never had any piano lessons. He did get a few tips later from Count Basie and from Willie "The Lion" Smith.

As Cockrell reports, Benjamin finished public elementary school with high grades, attended Sumner High School in western Kansas City, and eventually went on to Wilberforce University, a predominantly African-American junior college in Ohio. On June 2, 1927, he graduated with excellent grades, and a letter in varsity football.

After about two years, he returned to Kansas City, determined to become a musician. He had become a pretty good stride pianist by now. Some of his role models were Fats Waller, Duke Ellington, Willie "The Lion" Smith, Count Basie, and Rusty Nelson, a less well-known pianist working in Kansas City at the time. The brand-new pianist soon found work playing in all kinds of bars. He played solo much of the time, but also founded several small bands, including one with the notable name of Rooster Ben and His Little Red Hens.

Kansas City, of course, had a dynamic jazz scene then.

Because of cooperation between local authorities and the underworld, prohibition was entirely ignored. The economic crisis was taking place elsewhere, and bars had no closing times. In the Sunset Club, Ben's neighbor Pete Johnson played in a duo with a drummer. Joe Turner tended the bar and would sometimes sing the blues. Legend has it he did this without using a microphone, and without interrupting his work. The Sunset Club was one of the places where the legendary Kansas City jam sessions took place. The most popular club, however, was the Reno Club. This place had segregated areas for white and black visitors, cheap drinks, and the best orchestras. The owner, "Papa" Sol Epstein, had come to some agreements with authorities, so the police left them alone.

In 1927, at age 18 and still in college, Webster went on his first tour with Brethro Nelson and his combo. Shortly afterward, he traveled to Texas with Dutch Campbell's orchestra. According to trumpet player Rex Stewart, Webster's piano-playing skills in his maturity were not at a professional level.[7] But on two private recordings, probably from 1942, his playing sounds quite fluent, and even has some Art Tatum-like qualities. He plays the standard "Hallelujah," and his own composition "Deary."[8] Evidently he was a much better piano player when he was young than he was at a later age. The only commercially issued recordings with Ben Webster on piano, recorded in 1957 and 1964, tend to confirm this hypothesis.[9]

He always owned a piano—even during his Amsterdam

period—and he'd play for a few minutes every day without ever seriously working on his technique. Cees Slinger, who accompanied him in those days, remembered, "After a concert, if he was in a good mood, he'd sometimes sit down behind the piano. Stride piano. It wasn't the world's best piano music, but it would really swing. The bass player and drummer wouldn't accompany him when he got into this, because he always played only song fragments."

※

The first few orchestras in which Ben played piano didn't earn much of a living. The musicians toured shabby dance halls in a dilapidated bus. When food ran out they would stop the bus, and roll the dice to see which of the musicians would go and steal a chicken. Sometimes it was Ben's turn. He'd head off to a farm and twist a chicken's neck, after which they would roast it on a fire down the road.

It was during this period that he became interested in the saxophone. He had gotten curious after listening to Coleman Hawkins, solo player in Fletcher Henderson's orchestra at the time, and Frankie Trumbauer, a white player of the rare C-melody sax. Webster was also impressed by Johnny Hodges, Hilton Jefferson, and Benny Carter.

When Ben was working with Dutch Campbell in Amarillo, Texas, he met Budd Johnson, the sax player of Gene Coy's orchestra. Johnson later remembered that the young pianist had been crazy about Trumbauer.

"Ben wanted to learn saxophone. At the time Frankie Trumbauer was the baddest cat around. Everybody dug Frankie Trumbauer. He had recorded a solo on a tune called "Singin' the Blues" and everybody memorized the solo. Ben said to me, 'Hey man, l sure would like to learn to play that solo on the saxophone.' I said, 'First you got to learn to hold the thing.' "[10]

According to Webster, "I simply asked Budd one day, 'How do you play a scale on that thing of yours?' Budd showed me how to do that, and taught me a couple of riffs as well. I didn't know any more about it than that. In 1929, Lester Young's father came to Amarillo to pick up the pianist for his family orchestra, a guy named Harry Nelson. I asked him if he happened to need a saxophonist as well. He said he did, and then I told him, 'Fact is, I can't actually read music, Mr. Young.' This made him laugh, and he said, 'Well, I'll just have to teach you,' to which I replied, 'I think I should confess something else: I don't have an instrument.' He had a really good laugh at that, and said, 'Come on, get in the car. I'll handle that. I'll make sure you get an instrument as well."[11]

He rode to Albuquerque, New Mexico, with Billy Young's son Lester. He received daily lessons at the Youngs', borrowing Lester's sister Irma's alto saxophone for the time being.[12] He and Lester often played together, and Lester, who had been playing the saxophone for a few years by then, helped him out on the side.

It was during this time that Ben saved the lives of Lester and his younger brother Lee. The young members of the family orchestra would sometimes go swimming in the Rio Grande. One day, Lester was carried off by a strong current. Webster was a much better swimmer and, helped by guitar player Ted Brinson, he dragged him back to shore. At another time, Lee sank into a hole in the river bed. Lee: "I was drowning, and I'd just gone under for the last time! I was just a little boy, about ten or eleven years old, and he simply grabbed me under one arm and carried me home. He was a large guy by that time, you should have seen that body of his!"[13]

After as little as three months with the Young family, Ben was invited to join Gene Coy's orchestra. Another three months later, Coy's tenorist left. "I asked Gene if I could play the tenor. He said OK, and together we went to Uncle John, you know, a pawn shop, and bought a tenor. That was kind of a bad instrument, but a while later, Gene made sure I got a brand new tenor, paid in installments. That was in Oklahoma City."[14] Webster later would say: "I think I couldn't express myself on alto. The tenor had a bigger sound."[15]

notes

1 Henk Romijn Meijer, *Een Blauwe Golf aan de Kust* (Meulenhoff 1986).
2 From the movie *Big Ben*, by Johan van der Keuken (1967).
3 From the movie *The Brute and the Beautiful*, by John Jeremy (1989).
4 From the movie *Ballad for Ben*, by Per Moller Hansen.
5 From the movie *The Brute and the Beautiful*, by John Jeremy (1989).
6 See note 3.
7 Rex Stewart, *Jazzmasters of the 30's* (Macmillan Publishing

Co., a collection of articles from the 1970s), 121.

8 Never released on record.

9 Ben Webster, *Soulville* (Verve 833 551 3 CD); and Milt Hinton, *Here Swings the Judge* (Famous Door HL-104 LP).

10 Mike Zwerin, *Close Enough for Jazz* (Quartet Books 1983).

11 Bert Vuijsje, *Jazzportretten* (Van Gennep 1983).

12 Stanley Dance, *The World of Duke Ellington* (Schribner's 1970/1981).

13 *Jazz Journal*, January 1961.

14 See note 11.

15 *Down Beat*, June 26, 1958.

henderson, calloway, and wilson

Ben Webster was now beginning to make a name for himself as a sax player, and he played in ever-better orchestras. He worked for Jap Allen (1930), Blanche Calloway (1931), Bennie Moten (1931–1933), Andy Kirk (1933), Fletcher Henderson (1934), Benny Carter (1934), Willie Bryant (1935), Cab Calloway (1936–1937), Henderson again (1937–1938), and finally Duke Ellington (1940–1943). He'd worked together with Ellington on two previous studio sessions, in 1935 and 1936, but not yet on a permanent basis. He was also part of Duke's orchestra for a few weeks in 1935, when clarinet/tenor player Barney Bigard was on vacation.[1]

You can follow his development quite well through his recordings. With Blanche Calloway he sounds like an amateur; during his period with Moten he became a professional; in Henderson's orchestras he refined his professional work; and he finally became a musical personality as Ellington's sideman. In the fifties, playing in all kinds of small ensembles, he found his definitive personal style.

In March, May, and June of 1931, he made his first album recordings, with the orchestra of vaudeville singer Blanche Calloway, Cab's sister. He had been playing the sax for two years by then, and his performance varied from pathetic to barely acceptable. While he at least sounds like a mediocre Coleman Hawkins' acolyte on "Without That Gal," his solo in "Misery"—a fitting title, by the way—doesn't even meet minimal amateur standards. He has such a hard time simply getting a sound out of his instrument that he doesn't have any energy left to develop nice ideas.[2]

Most of his work from the thirties sounds very dated now. He didn't have many models, as the tenor sax was still in its puberty up to the second world war. The instrument was often played using a curious vibrato and glissandi that impart an overly sentimental quality. Even Coleman Hawkins, Ben's main role model, is found using this technique on occasion. One of the most horrifying examples of pre-war saxophone music is Prince Robinson's (1902–1960) solo, recorded February 18, 1937 on "The Mood I'm In." With his goat-like vibrato, Robinson sounds like a grotesque parody of contemporary Hawkins disciples—even though he was no doubt deadly serious.[3] Musicians had great respect for him; he was considered Hawkins' equal. According to Budd Johnson, Webster copied some of the solos Robinson made in Jap Allen's band.

It is interesting to note that Lester Young's supple, seemingly uncomplicated solos have stood the test of time remarkably well. Young's first solos on record—the

"Shoe Shine Boy" session from 1936—don't sound the least bit dated. But if anyone today were to play in the style favored by Hawkins' epigones, they would definitely get some funny looks. Hawkins was developing faster than his students, but he lived in Europe between 1934 and 1939, and few of his recordings made it to the United States.

Webster was of course familiar with Lester Young's work; the two of them had studied together, after all. "I was amazed that Lester already played so well back then [1929]. I liked his style, but Coleman Hawkins had always been my favorite. He had a heavier tone, and I liked just about everything he played."[4] Webster was certainly not the only tenor player who favored Hawkins; it wasn't until the forties that Young's approach became popular.

⋇

At the end of 1931, Ben moved to Bennie Moten's orchestra, based in Kansas City. This band was really the precursor of Count Basie's big band; after Moten's death on April 2, 1935, band pianist Basie took over the helm. In the only record session Bennie Moten made with Webster, on December 13, 1932, the typical Basie sound isn't yet there. The wind section's ensemble work is imprecise, important forces like drummer Jo Jones and guitarist Freddie Green were not yet hired, and Basie plays the piano with both hands simultaneously.[5]

The tenor player, however, sounds remarkably fluid for someone who had played the sax now for only three years. His tone has improved, and he has developed an impressive fleet-fingeredness. But he generally tends to play too many notes—it sounds like his main goal is to become the world's fastest sax player. There are some mitigating circumstances, however: the tempo on these sessions was usually quite fast.

In pictures, Moten's big band looks spectacular, but in reality the band had a hard time getting by. A tour to the East Coast ended in disaster. Sax player Eddie Barefield remembers: "We were stranded in nearly every city on our way to New York... We just hung around the town until they got another raggedy bus. All those buses were always breaking down!... Being stranded meant that you were in a town without work or money. You had to eat and sleep, but you couldn't get out. Bennie [Moten] might hustle up enough to get us a meal ticket."[6]

Barefield recalls the circumstances of the aforementioned record session with Moten. The group had played in Philadelphia, but hadn't been paid. Barefield was forced to pawn his suit and his clarinet. "We had to get to Camden [New Jersey] to record, and along comes this little guy Archie with a raggedy old bus, and he took us there. He got us a rabbit and four loaves of bread, and we cooked rabbit stew right on a pool table. That kept us from starving, and then we went on to make the records."[7]

In spite of all the obstacles, Moten and his men finally made it to New York. Once there, their living conditions improved somewhat. Webster befriended some local musicians. With drummer Sid Catlett and trumpet player Rex Stewart he formed a kind of mini-sports club,

The Big Three. They swam in the Lido Pool on Seventh Avenue, which was popular with artists, then would go on bike rides or play basketball. Webster still had a car in those days, a Buick, and he would drive Catlett and Stewart home after these activities. In the fifties, Ben stopped driving altogether, probably because of his drinking problem.

In 1933 he returned to Kansas City, to play in Andy Kirk's orchestra in Fairyland Park. No records were made in this period, even though it must have been quite a good band. The pianist was Mary Lou Williams, someone he got along with very well. The two apparently never developed a romance—rumors to the contrary—because she was still close to her first husband, John Williams. Webster also went on tour with Kirk's orchestra, which could be hired for forty-five dollars a night. The tenor player recalled: "We'd drive into a town and ask a filling station man where the ballroom was where we were to play. Then Mouse [trumpeter Irving Randolph] would drive up to within a block of the spot. We'd all get out, comb our hair and straighten our clothes, and walk casually over to the spot as if we were going from our hotel. About the time we got there Mouse would drive up in the truck, saluting to us, and unloading the horns. Mouse would always put on a big taxi driver's cap after he let us out so he would look like a big-time chauffeur when he drove up. Man, those were the days."[8]

It was no wonder that a lot of orchestras preferred to remain in Kansas City, as there was a lot of work available for jazz musicians. The neighborhood was controlled by Tom Pendergast, the local Democratic party leader. Pendergast had come to power through election fraud and corruption, and maintained lucrative connections with the underworld. The city's nightlife was booming during his administration, and (as mentioned earlier) there was plenty of latitude for marginal phenomena like drinking, jazz, and prostitution. During the first two decades of the century his power was considerable; after he positioned Henry McElroy to manage the city for him in 1931, his power was absolute.

It wasn't until 1938 that the law caught up with Pendergast, who was almost seventy years old by that time. He was sentenced to fifteen months in prison when income tax fraud of more than half a million dollars came to light. This marked the end of his reign, and the local jazz scene collapsed along with him.

Although jazz musicians had an easier time finding work in Kansas City than elsewhere, that didn't mean their life was easy. Pay was low, the nights were long, and the famous clubs were in reality no more than ramshackle saloons. The Basie Band played in the Reno Club from ten at night to five in the morning, at a weekly salary of fourteen dollars a man. This didn't stop musicians from having a good time, however—after a night's work, a lot of them would continue to jam until ten or eleven AM.

The countless jam sessions made for some healthy competition. Webster and Hawkins met one legendary night in the Cherry Blossom Club on December 18, 1933, when Hawkins was in Kansas City with Fletcher

Henderson. Mary Lou Williams' account of this occasion has been quoted numerous times: "The date must have been early 1934, because Prohibition had been lifted and whiskey was freely on sale... The word went round that Hawkins was in the Cherry Blossom, and within about half an hour there were Lester Young, Ben Webster, Herschel Evans, Herman Walder, and one or two unknown tenors piling in the club to blow. Bean didn't know the Kaycee tenor men were so terrific, and he couldn't get himself together though he played all morning. I happened to be nodding that night, and around four AM, I awoke to hear someone pecking on my screen. I opened the window on Ben Webster. He was saying, 'Get up, pussycat, we're jammin' and all the pianists are tired out now. Hawkins has got his shirt off and is still blowing. You got to come down.' Sure enough, when we got there, Hawkins was in his singlet, taking turns with the Kaycee men. It seems he had run into something he hadn't expected. Lester's style was light, and, as I said, it took him maybe five choruses to warm up. But then he could really blow; then you couldn't handle him on a cutting session.

"That was how Hawkins got hung up. The Henderson band was playing in St. Louis that evening, and Bean knew he ought to be on the way. But he kept trying to blow something to beat Ben and Herschel and Lester. When at last he gave up, he got straight in his car and drove to St. Louis. I heard he'd just bought a new Cadillac and that he burnt it out trying to make the job on time. Yes, Hawkins was king until he met those crazy

Kansas City tenor men."[9]

Bass player Gene Ramey: "The adage in Kansas City was, and still is: *Say something on your horn*—don't just show off your versatility and ability to execute. *Tell us a story, and don't let it be a lie.* Let it *mean* something.[10]

※

In July 1934, Webster had progressed enough to inherit his idol's place in Henderson's orchestra. The original replacement, Lester Young, had quit after a short time. The Henderson musicians preferred a player out of the Hawkins school, with a heavy tone and lots of vibrato. They couldn't have made a better choice than Webster: "I had heard all of Hawkins' records and I'd studied them all, and it was quite an experience taking his chair."[12] Journalist John Hammond wrote: "Fletcher now has a new tenor saxophonist, Lester Young having returned to the Andy Kirk band in Kansas City. This new saxophonist is Ben Webster, and I hold him in very high esteem. Beautiful tone and good musicianship. There is still only one Hawkins, however."[13]

Henderson's orchestra was no more than a notch below Duke Ellington's. The rhythm section was much more nimble than most, and the arrangements were complicated, especially for that era. In the September 1934 recordings, songs like "Happy as the Day Is Long" and "Tidal Wave" display dazzling reed work, accompanied by a light, supple background supplied by Elmer James on bass and Walter Johnson on drums.[14]

The new tenor player had only been playing the sax for

opposite: with Fletcher Henderson, 1937

five years, and this new gig threw him into the deep end. "I was actually scared to play in that orchestra, because I knew that the music they played was incredibly difficult... The band played in every key imaginable. It's thanks to my good friend [reed player] Russell Procope that I got to stay in that orchestra. He helped me out tremendously by studying together with me."[15]

Henderson gave his tenor player a lot of room to solo, and Webster quickly became one of the better tenor players. His tone deepened, and his playing grew in confidence. Unfortunately, he still played too many notes and, like virtually all tenors at the time, retained that awkward vibrato. But first trumpeter Russell Smith taught him something essential. "He taught me to be tone-conscious. I had played in the band for a few days, and mainly tried to play as fast as possible. He said, 'You're sitting next to [reeds] Russell Procope and Buster Bailey and Hilton Jefferson, and all you are trying to do is play fast. You've got quite a nice tone—why don't you try to do something with that instead?' I never forgot that, and immediately started working on my tone."[16]

He would probably have stayed with Henderson longer if financial trouble hadn't prevented it. Henderson was a good-natured fellow, but no businessman. In November 1934, the orchestra disintegrated, and Henderson went on to write arrangements for Benny Goodman. Duke Ellington described the break-up: "Work was scarce, but the band was so fine, and the guys so attached to it, that nobody had the heart to quit... Finally, when they couldn't hang out any longer, the whole band got together, and everybody turned in their notice at the same time."[17]

Henderson's agent had been Irving Mills, who gave all the good gigs to Ellington and Cab Calloway. He considered Henderson's orchestra second-rate, so they had to make do with what was left over. Trumpeter Mouse Randolph was amazed at how the orchestra leader managed to play on even the most out-of-tune pianos—if necessary, he would simply transpose his parts to a different key, while his orchestra members played their parts as usual.[18]

After Henderson's orchestra broke up, Benny Carter and some of Henderson's musicians made a record in 1934. It included "Dream Lullaby," the song that featured Webster's first mature ballad solo.[19] Webster went on to make some freelance recordings with singer Willie Bryant, which further document his progress—his timing and tone have become excellent on "Voice of the Old Man River."[20] Actually, his solos with Ellington in 1935 and 1936—"In a Jam" and "Truckin' "—are not nearly as impressive.[21]

※

According to his second cousin Joyce and cousin Harley, Ben's drinking and short temper often got him into trouble during this period. As Harley wrote to me, "After a fight, Ben once pushed a girl out of a window at the Dunbar Hotel in Los Angeles, back in 1936. I can't remember what caused the fight." The woman survived the fall, but must have been injured. According to Joyce, Duke Ellington—in whose orchestra Ben had played a few times by then—intervened on Ben's behalf to keep him from going to jail. Ben never talked about the incident. Aside from Harley and Joyce, nobody else I spoke with—even Jimmy Rowles and Harold Ashby, Ben's best friends in the States—had heard of it. Dan Morgenstern of the Institute of Jazz Studies agreed to ask a few Ellington researchers, but his inquiries didn't yield any results. There are no documents, either, that even mention it. Perhaps Ellington and Ben's family succeeded in keeping the matter out of the papers. If the incident really did occur, Ben's career does not seem to have been adversely affected.

※

Webster moved to Cab Calloway's orchestra in 1936, probably the most popular and best-paid black orchestra in the thirties. He acted like a seasoned musician—that is, he drank heavily, and favored expensive suits that made his shoulders look even broader than they were. When he wasn't playing, he spent most of his time in gambling halls and whorehouses. Fellow musicians only knew him in this incarnation, so he had achieved his goal: nobody was ever going to call him a sissy again.

According to Rex Stewart, "Nobody seeing Ben hang out on the corner of Forty-seventh and South Park, or Eighteenth and Vine, or at the Braddock Bar in Harlem would ever suspect that he was anything other than a corner roustabout. His yelling and laughing fit right into the picture, as did his attire. His high-priced shoes were just like those affected by gamblers, hustlers, and pimps, while his expensive hats were worn cocked in such a manner that they were a blatant gesture of defiance to the conventional world."[22]

In 1936, bass player Milt Hinton also joined Calloway's band. Hinton was an unknown young man, and a modest dresser. When he first entered the orchestra's reserved Pullman train wagon, Webster was nowhere to be found. He and the band leader had gone out to explore the local nightlife, had missed the train, and had to hurry to catch up it at a station further down the line.

They came stumbling up the gangway, and noticed Hinton sitting there. According to Hinton, "Ben looked at me, and he said, 'What is *that*?' And Cab Calloway said, 'That is the new bass player.' And Ben said, 'The new *what*?' Because I weighed about 115 pounds soaking wet, I had no decent clothes, I'd never played with a big band before, and I was making thirty-five dollars a week, and Cab Calloway was paying 100 bucks a week, so my qualifications were very, very low. But he [Ben] hadn't heard me play, and I said to myself, 'This is one man I would never, ever like.' And of course he became my dearest and best friend."[23]

Ben immediately decided it was time Hinton bought a new wardrobe; he didn't want to be seen in the company of such an unstylish dresser. The two went to a clothing store along with trombone player Keg Johnson, a colleague from the Calloway band. At the store, it was Webster and Johnson who made all the decisions—Hinton just stood by like an obedient little boy.

After a night's work, Webster would usually change out of his band uniform and into one of his flashy suits to jam at one of the local clubs. Hinton had to go along with him on these occasions, because a lesser bassist just wouldn't do. He reports that whenever the two of them went out, Ben would perform the same act: he'd enter the dark club and, while still in the doorway, would light a match to illuminate his face. Musicians would immediately start whispering, "Ben Webster is here!" He got a kick from the attention.[24]

One problem was that Calloway didn't allow his musicians much room for solos. Cab would sing his hits—"Smokey Joe," "Reefer Man," and "Minnie the Moocher," with the famous Hi-De-Ho chorus—and the orchestra would function merely as background. Webster kept up his inspiration by going out to jam, but he inevitably lost interest in this show orchestra after a time.

Hinton shared his feelings. "Cab was the star, and there was nothing else but Cab the star. The men sat there and made a hundred dollars a week, which was a tremendous amount of money in the thirties... It was, on average, more than Duke was paying in those days."[25]

The musical direction of Calloway's orchestra gradually changed when the band started playing at New York's Cotton Club in 1936. The club audience wanted to hear jazz, not just Calloway's show tunes. Cab's musicians were also regularly invited for record sessions. At first, the orchestra leader was vehemently opposed: "If I hear you guys going out making records, making somebody else great when you're working for me—whoever makes a date is fired!" Webster, however, resisted. "You should be ashamed of yourself. You should be honored that you've got men in your band everybody else wants. If you do what you said, you'll be interfering with my living, and you can get yourself another saxophone player."[26]

Calloway came to realize that his musicians deserved some attention as well. At the Cotton Club, a few instrumental pieces made it into the repertoire. These developments advanced especially during the tenure of Chu Berry, Webster's successor—solos were still short in Webster's time. For this reason, Ben's recordings with Calloway have little more than novelty value in the context of his complete oeuvre.

⋇

Webster had some superficial affairs during this period, the most sensational of which was with Billie Holiday. It was short-lived. At some point he gave her a black eye. Billie was used to worse from men, so she didn't make too big a deal of it. Her mother, on the other hand, was livid. The next time Ben went to pick Billie up at the New York apartment where she lived with her mother, he thought it best to stay in his car and honk to let her know he was waiting. He opened the car door to let her in, but didn't notice that Billie's mother had quietly followed behind. She was carrying an umbrella, and started beating on him, screaming about the worse beating she would give him if he ever dared touch her daughter again.

Ben recalls: "Naturally I could see that Billie's Ma was real mad, but what made it worse was that Billie was just busting with laughter at the sight of me being whupped. That made me mad, but we all ended up friends."[27] He seldom referred to the relationship later. In the sixties, he did tell his Amsterdam friend Dolf Verspoor that he had taken Billie home to Mayme and Mom one time when they both had to be there for work. It wasn't a very long visit—his mother and great aunt clearly didn't consider her a "lady." After a cold reception, Billie slipped away as soon as was convenient.

In her autobiography, *Lady Sings the Blues*, Billie doesn't mention the affair at all. "Roy Eldridge, Lester Young, Benny Webster—they were all friends of mine. But Benny Goodman was somebody special among the musicians I hung out with..."[28]

Webster broke off his lucrative gig with Calloway in July 1937, because he wanted to play with Duke Ellington. Ellington's orchestra didn't pay as well, but musically it excelled the other big bands. It was not until 1940, however, that he actually became Ellington's employee. According to Hinton, the two were brother bands: the leaders had an agreement never to hire away the other's important soloists. This meant a hiatus of some years before anyone could jump to the other outfit.

In the meantime, Ben returned to the re-established Fletcher Henderson big band. He replaced Chu Berry there, who in turn had left to play for Calloway. In this period, Henderson's orchestra continued to struggle. Rex Stewart, not someone given to critical comments, complained that the band leader was so mild-mannered that he was simply unable to assert himself when the situation called for it.[29] Discipline was almost entirely absent; musicians sometimes drank too much, came to work too late, or missed rehearsals. Webster left Henderson in May or June of 1938, a year before his band folded for a second time. Henderson then got a permanent position as Benny Goodman's arranger. A few years later he made another brief attempt to hold an orchestra together, but Ben was not part of this lineup.

The sax player played in a number of large and small ensembles, until pianist Teddy Wilson made him an offer in 1939. He wanted to start his own big band, with Ben playing a central role. Ben later claimed that "I played all the solos in that orchestra—the band was built around me." This is partially confirmed on the records Wilson's orchestra made: excepting Wilson and the vocalist, Webster plays the majority of solos.

The two had played together in several studio formations since 1935. These recordings have been largely reissued under Billie Holiday's name.[30] The tenor solos in these recordings are not without merit, but a little archaic. Webster's performance in "Pennies From Heaven" and "I Can't Give You Anything But Love" are marred by outdated ideas about tone formation, including the peculiar, bleating vibrato. But on "Too Hot For Words" and "What a Night, What a Moon, What a Girl," his playing is very confident and robust, despite the fast tempo. These solos point forward to the playing of the "heavy tenors" who became so popular after World War II.

The studio recordings made by Wilson's big band are not exactly inspiring. Webster shows definite signs of a personal style in songs like "Some Other Spring," but the solos are generally too short and the arrangements not very stimulating. The rhythm section is mediocre—despite J.C. Heard's involvement—and Thelma Carpenter and Jean Eldridge's vocals sound old-fashioned today.[31]

Some live recordings by the same orchestra, however, include an excellent chorus on "Exactly Like You," and some sultry sounds on "The Man I Love." The rhythm section appears to be in much better form here, and Wilson's solo is of an Art Tatum-like virtuosity.[32]

In 1939, Webster was present at another session headed by Lionel Hampton, but he played only a subordinate role owing to the wealth of other talent, including Benny Carter, Coleman Hawkins, Chu Berry, Charlie Christian, and Hampton himself.[33]

Wilson's band was never a commercial success. Webster seems to have believed that the underworld was responsible for the band's demise. In an interview in Amsterdam with Bert Vuijsje and Simon Korteweg, thirty years later and a continent away, he said cryptically, "I heard from all kinds of people in the business that the orchestra's future was limited." Vuijsje: "In a whisper, urging us never to tell a soul, he indicated that by these 'all kinds of people in the business' he meant the mafia, who for some reason had decided that Wilson's big band should not become successful."[34]

Guitar player Arie Ligthart worked together for months

with Teddy Wilson (1912–1986) on an autobiography. Based on these interviews, Ligthart reports: "Oh, the mafia had nothing to do with that. You can take my word for it—it was Teddy's own fault. He was no businessman. He was a partygoer, a jazz fanatic and a scatterbrain. Definitely not the type to head an orchestra like that. Giving shows, playing a commercially viable repertoire—that didn't interest him in the least. He just pumped a lot of money into that orchestra, became aware that it wasn't going anywhere, and then simply gave up. In his book, Teddy openly discusses the mafia, but he makes no connection whatsoever between organized crime and his band's downfall."[35]

notes

1 In the May 1965 issue of *Jazz Magazine*, Webster said that he was replacing Otto Hardwick who was on vacation. However, Hardwick did not play tenor. Incidentally, Bigard and Hardwick also both play on Webster's first two record sessions with Ellington.

2 *The Essential Blanche Calloway*, Le Jazz Classics.

3 *The Quintessential Billie Holiday*, Vol. 1–3 (Columbia).

4 Bert Vuijsje, *Jazzportretten* (Van Gennep 1983).

5 Bennie Moten: *Basie Beginnings*, RCA. Also on Classics.

6 Stanley Dance, *The World of Count Basie* (Charles Scribner's Sons 1980).

7 Ross Russell, *Jazz Style in Kansas City and the Southwest* (University of California Press 1971).

8 Marshall Stearns, *The Story of Jazz* (Oxford University Press 1956).

9 Nat Shapiro and Nat Hentoff (edd.), *Hear Me Talkin' to Ya* (Penguin Books 1955/1966), 292–293.

10 See note 7.

11 See note 9.

12 *Down Beat*, October 5, 1955.
13 *Jazz Tango*, July 13, 1934.
14 *Fletcher Henderson and his Orchestra 1932–1934*, Classics.
15 See note 4.
16 See note 4.
17 See note 9.
18 Walter C. Allen, *Hendersonia*, self-published in 1973.
19 *Benny Carter 1933–1936*, Classics.
20 *Willie Bryant 1935–1936*, Classics.
21 *Duke Ellington 1935–1936* and *D.E, 1936–1937*, Classics.
22 Rex Stewart, *Jazzmasters of the 30's* (Macmillan Publishing Co., a collection of articles from the 1970s).
23 From the film *The Brute and the Beautiful*, by John Jeremy (1989).
24 See note 23.
25 Stanley Dance, *The World of Swing* (Charles Schribner's Sons 1974).
26 See note 25.
27 John Chilton, *Billie's Blues* (Quartet books 1956).
28 Billie Holiday and William Dufty, *Lady Sings the Blues* (Doubleday 1956).
29 See note 22.
30 *The Billie Holiday Story, vol. 1*, CBS; see also note 3.
31 *Teddy Wilson and His Big Band*, Tax M-80 18 (LP).
32 *Teddy Wilson 1939*, Classics.
33 *Three Great Swing Saxophones* (RCA NL 90405 CD).
34 *Jazz Nu*, January 1980.
35 Teddy Wilson, *Teddy Wilson Talks Jazz* (University of Michigan Press 1992, Arie Ligthart and Humphrey van Loo, edd.).

with the guv'nor: duke ellington

I really started to develop my own sound in 1938. That was when I was with Stuff Smith, as I recall. I used to have a bunch of Hawk's records and a record player with me all the time. I would wake up in the morning and listen to Hawk. One day, a guy [probably pianist Clyde Hart] said to me, 'Well, Ben, you finally did it.' I asked him what he meant. He said, 'You sound just like Hawk now.' I packed up the record player and took it to Kansas City for my folks. From then on, I developed on my own."[1]

Under Ellington's wing, Ben Webster became Ben Webster. His tone slowly broke free of the Hawkins sound. Hawkins' tone was brassy and domineering, Webster's warmer and gentler. Influenced by Johnny Hodges, Ellington's lead alto, he learned to slide up to a note from below. The influence of Hodges' melodious delivery was also becoming evident. In the ballads "Until Tonight" and "I Hear a Rhapsody," you can hear a mixture of Hodges' techniques, Ben's future personal style, and just a small relic of Hawkins' influence.[2]

Webster begn to play fewer notes. His solos became

more melodious. He started thinking "horizontally" (i.e., in phrases) rather than "vertically" (running through all the changes). His sense of form became more refined. Hawkins sometimes had trouble finding a good ending for his improvisations. Webster's best solos, on the other hand, sound like rounded compositions. His famous solo in "Cotton Tail" is a good example. Every phrase is in the right place, there isn't a note too many, the construction is seamless, and the beginning and end are distinctive.[3]

In general, Ben tried to project a relaxed attitude. It was important to keep the music lively, but the result should never sound rushed. Hawkins preferred to play every note possible, didn't like to skip any transitional chords, and in general gave the impression that he didn't care to let a single opportunity go by. Webster's work from this period sounds casual and unaffected by comparison. By letting all kinds of opportunities pass, he creates more tension. He increases his dramatic power through a plain approach, where every action is in service to the form and atmosphere.

By preference, his solos were in moderate tempos and ballads. Ellington (reverently christened "The Guv'nor" by Webster) allowed him to play solos in the slower pieces right from the start, showing how well he knew which musician to associate with a particular style of music. The lazy "Just A-Settin' And A-Rockin' " seemed tailor-made for Webster.[4]

The tenor player also thrived on the ballad "All Too Soon," the slowly rippling "Chloe," and "Mobile Bay," a slow blues that he recorded with a small group of

Ellington musicians led by Rex Stewart. An excellent recording from this period is "Lament for Javanette," where his broad sound really stands out (thanks in part to the recording's good sound quality).[5] Webster also developed into a better band musician. Just like the other Ellingtonians, he'd train his musical memory night after night, learning to play the arrangements by head. "Johnny and Rex and the rest of us would learn our parts quick as we could, because mostly everyone in the band got it that way. Then we'd sit in the band and play all night without ever opening the book."[6]

In the summer of 1941, Hawkins—who had returned from Europe—was asked to list his favorite tenor players. Webster ranked at the top of the list. Hawkins praised Lester Young for his originality, and Chu Berry for his speed and knowledge of harmony, but, "Webster has the best and biggest sound. His phrasing is excellent too."[7]

It is evident why Webster considered his time with Ellington of great importance, even if it only lasted three-and-a-half years. He considered them the best years of his life, and his entire career was defined in terms of it. Before his Ellington period, he was the tenor player who was trying to get into his orchestra; after he left, he was identified first and foremost as an Ellington veteran. According to Harold Ashby (who replaced Ben in Ellington's orchestra), "Duke was his whole life."

※

Late January, 1940, the big moment finally arrived. "Jonesy [Ellington's band boy] came over one day to tell me Ellington wanted to see me. I immediately felt twenty years younger. I was drunk at the time, but the news sobered me up in a second... After Jonesy had come to get me, I went to see Ellington in the dressing room of the theater where he was playing at the time. He said, 'Why don't you come to the rehearsal tomorrow morning?'

"Then I realized I'd have to tell Teddy Wilson that I was leaving him. To be able to do that, I had to get drunk all over again... 'Wilson,' I said—we called each other Wilson and Webster—'I really don't know how to tell you this. I've just had this ambition to play for the Guv'nor for years.' Years later, Teddy told me, 'Webster, you made the right decision.' I just about begged him for that job. Those were the best days of my life. Once you've played for Ellington, that's something you'll carry with you forever."[8]

It took him a while to get used to the sometimes dissonant harmonies, which were very advanced for that time. "Whenever they gave me a new piece of music, I'd sometimes be afraid to play certain notes at full volume, because they sounded so strange. Juan Tizol, the valve trombone player, noticed this one day, and told me: 'Just go ahead and play them, because that's the way Duke likes it... When you're standing in front of the orchestra, they will sound good after all.' "[9]

He became the fifth man in the reed section, which introduced the convention of the five-man reed section. The others were Barney Bigard (clarinet), Johnny Hodges and Otto Hardwick (alto sax), and Harry Carney

Opposite: a publicity still from the film "Cabin in the Sky" (1943) with Ellington's orchestra; Webster is seen leaning on the piano

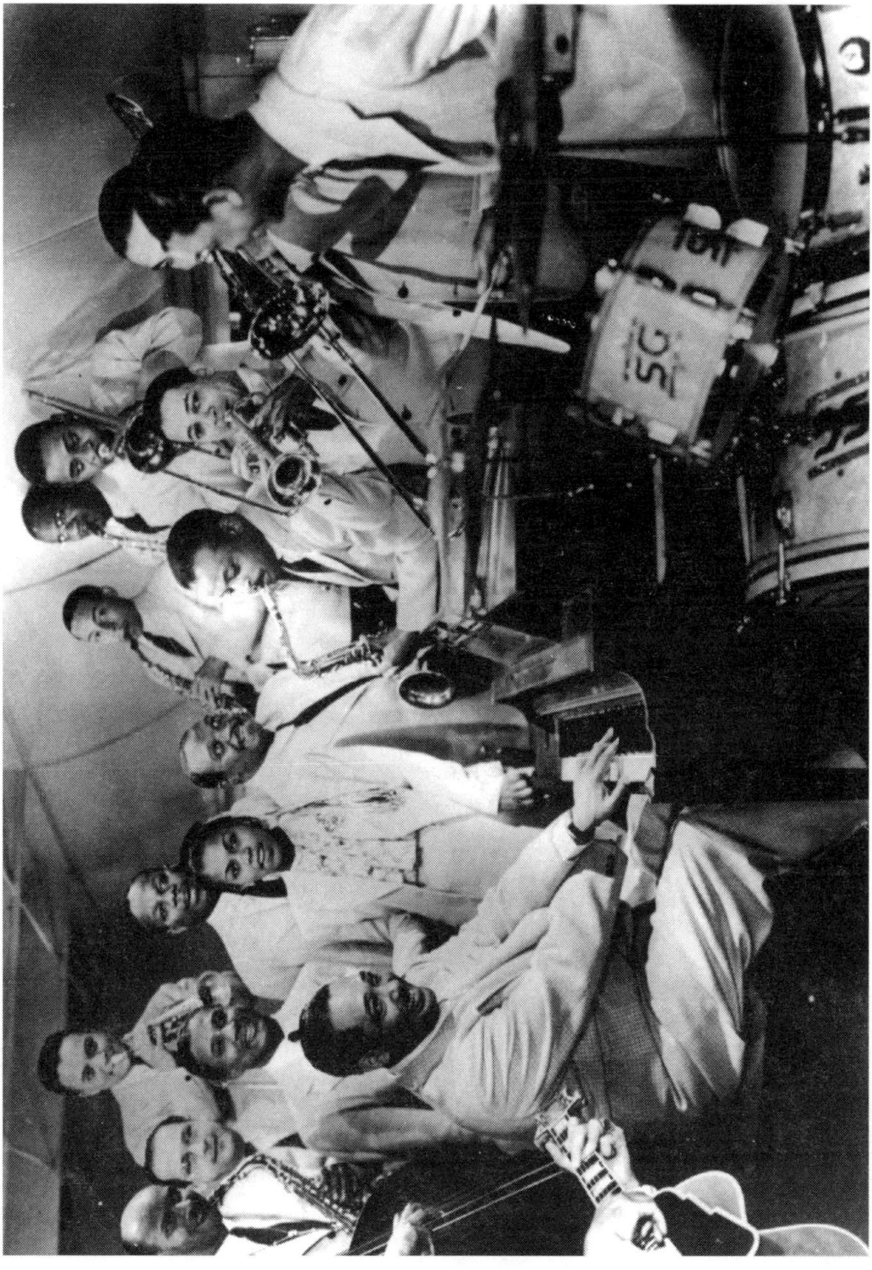

(baritone sax). All these musicians would play "doubles" when necessary—Hodges, for instance, sometimes played the clarinet or soprano sax. Webster was the only one given the privilege of playing one instrument exclusively.

This lineup remained unchanged until June of 1942, when Benny Bigard left the orchestra. His position was temporarily filled by Jimmy Hamilton, who sometimes had to play the tenor in arrangements. Hamilton didn't like this. "Clarinet was my instrument, but on saxophone I was more of an alto player. That didn't matter to him."[10] As Bigard wasn't crazy about the tenor either, Webster was now not just the best, but in fact the only tenor soloist in the orchestra.

He became the standard for Ellington tenor players. When Paul Gonsalves joined the band in 1950, he knew several of his predecessor's solos by heart. "I've got this job, because l know all Ben Webster's solos from the records... The first thing Duke played was "C Jam Blues" and then "Just A-Settin' and A-Rockin'." So I asked him if he still had "Chelsea Bridge," and as I stood up to play my solo I overheard him say to Quentin Jackson: 'This so-and-so sounds just like Ben!' So I got the job."[11] Harold Ashby, who joined full time in 1968 after a few gigs with the band, also acknowledged his influence. "After I heard Ben, he was my main inspiration on tenor."[12]

As noted earlier, Webster had been influenced by Hodges' lyricism. However, Carney's vigorous tone also left its mark. "You talk about sound... Carney was at one end of that saxophone team and I was at the other. And

I tried to blend with him. We used to run Duke mad, me and Harry Carney. Duke would say: 'Cut it out fellers, I can't hear anyone else.' I say Pops [Russell Smith, Henderson's first trumpeter] made me tone-conscious and that section did the rest."[13]

※

Webster's greatest hit was "Cotton Tail," a fast number played over the chords of "I Got Rhythm." It's odd that this piece became so popular, since Webster generally didn't favor fast tempos. There's an anecdote Ben liked to tell about the origin of the classic "Cotton Tail" solo—a solo Ellington always made the tenorist repeat precisely, note for note.[14]

On the night of May 3, 1940, he had gone out with Ellington, at the leader's invitation. Alcohol flowed freely. The next morning Duke woke him up early, telling him there would be a record session that morning. After Webster arrived at the studio, hung over from the night before, Ellington told the recording technicians to start the tape. He then said to the musicians, "We'll play through the piece once, just for the notes."

The tenor player was furious when he found out that everything had been recorded; he hadn't had the chance to do what he intended. Later on, however, he had to admit that Ellington was right: this carefully constructed improvisation represented some of his best work ever.[15]

But is this how it actually happened? When he told Bert Vuijsje this story in the sixties, he placed the incident in Chicago. He also mentioned a hotel and a club in that town in connection with the story. According to all reliable discographies, however, the recording took place in Hollywood.

Wherever it took place, the meaning of the story is clear. Webster had only been with the orchestra a few months, and still had to divest himself of Hawkins' baroque style. He knew that Ellingon had to resort to this trick to make him think it was only a test pressing, and get him to perform in a more relaxed manner.

In the event, what he produced was a solo with great variation: phrases with eighth notes, interrupted by notes that are suddenly longer, performed with a sound that ranges from a whisper to a furious roar. In the first eight measures of the second chorus he seems to ignore the chords—bass player Jimmie Blanton simply holds a B flat as a pedal tone.

⁂

On several occasions, the tenor player said that his best concert with Ellington was the one in the Crystal Ballroom in Fargo, North Dakota, on November 7, 1940. This concert was taped by two fans, Jack Towers and Dick Burris, and a large part of it is now available on two CDs.[16]

It was very cold in the hall. "It was so cold there that night, we played in our overcoats, and some of the guys kept their gloves on."[17] In spite of this, the orchestra was in good shape, and the atmosphere was informal and relaxed. The high point of the night was "Stardust." Ben had the floor for a full four-and-a-half minutes, in a moderately slow dance tempo. The tenor player starts with a sultry, muffled sound, and gradually grows more

Duke Ellington orchestra in Sioux Falls, July 1939. Front row: Bigard, Hodges, Hardwick, Webster, Carney; back row: Stewart, Nance, W. Jones, Greer, Nanton, Tizol, Brown.

aggressive. There is a minimalist arrangement for the wind section (written by Webster himself, with some help from Blanton), but most of the recording simply features Webster's tenor. He may have been inspired by Hawkins' famous version of "Body and Soul," recorded a year earlier.

"Body and Soul," incidentally, was never part of Ben's regular repertoire. "There's nothing else to play on this tune—Bean straightened that one out... I detest a request to play this tune."[18]

※

Ellington's new sax player was a popular guy. According to Ellington's son Mercer, he always managed to create a "brotherly atmosphere." He just could not accept that these big bands tended to consist of a collection of individuals who'd each go their own way after the show. Drummer Roy Haynes, who substituted at some point: "The guys of Ellington's band were pretty hard to approach... Ben Webster was an exception—he was always hanging around with the pimps and the hookers."[19]

Webster didn't hesitate to use his physical power to help out his friends, which resulted in some legendary scenes. Jimmy Hamilton once got into trouble with a sailor because he was talking to a white girl. Webster joined the group, quickly assessed the situation, and punched the sailor out.

His best friend was the very young bassist Jimmie Blanton, who had been working for Ellington for a few months longer than he. Ben later admitted to his shock when he first spotted Blanton at a rehearsal. He greatly admired the previous bass player, Billy Taylor, and he had never heard of this kid. Ellington gave him some sound advice: "Maybe you should listen to him first."[20]

Webster's story contradicts Ellington's report in his autobiography *Music Is My Mistress*, that he and Webster discovered the new bass player together, along with Strayhorn. Blanton had been playing for the orchestra before Webster even joined. As a result of this confusion, some books still claim that Webster started playing for Ellington in 1939.

It hardly needs mentioning that Blanton was one of the pioneers of the modern bass. He played fluent, melodic lines, and with more swing than his predecessors in Ellington's band. Blanton's playing—especially in the second duo session with Ellington—contains runs that nowadays are still being used by Ray Brown, with great success.[21] Unfortunately, Blanton's rhythmic suppleness was often offset by drummer Sonny Greer's rigid timekeeping.

Blanton's knowledge of harmony was much greater than was common for the time. Webster said, "I would often ask him questions about chord changes, and he'd know the answer almost all the time. I had a hard time with the scheme in "Take the 'A' Train," for instance. 'What's that second chord?' I asked the Bear [Blanton]. 'Augmented,' he said, 'you would probably call that the whole-tone scale...'

" 'Bear, where do you get all this stuff?' I once asked him. He said his uncle taught him all that. Later on, I ended up meeting his uncle at Bear's home in Chattanooga, Tennessee. He was a short fellow who didn't utter so much as ten words a day. 'Is that the uncle you were talking about?' I asked Bear. 'He don't look like nothin' to me.' But Bear insisted that that was him. I guess that just goes to show that still waters run deep."[22]

Pianist Jimmy Rowles got to know Blanton and Webster when the two worked with Ellington in Seattle for a few weeks. Rowles was in his early 20s then. "Every night, I'd play with them in after hours sessions at clubs. I didn't know what was happening to me—I had never played with musicians this good. Jimmie was a really sweet, quiet kid. A living doll. All the band members and everyone in Seattle was crazy about him."

It was the fashion among jazz musicians to give each other nicknames back then. Webster, not about to be outdone by anyone, christened the skinny 21-year-old bass player with the odd name "Bear." The name Blanton thought up for Webster was more fitting: "Frog." His large, slightly bulging eyes, often emphasized by large bags underneath, gave him an undeniably frog-like appearance.

After a fight with his wife that left him broke, Milt Hinton—or "Fump," in Webster's dictionary—visited Ben at the Braddock Hotel in Harlem in 1940. He had every right to call on Ben, as the latter had borrowed money from him on many occasions "Ben was always in trouble, drinking and getting broke. I was trying to be conservative, and I would try to hold onto my money. Ben would come and get money from my wife Mona."[23]

opposite: Ellington singer Ivie Anderson and bassist Jimmy Blanton, 1941

After he had waited for about an hour, Webster and Blanton entered the hotel bar. It turned out all the tenor player had on him was some change. Hinton writes, "I remember, he turned to Blanton who was standing at the bar about ten feet away and said, 'Bear, come over here.'

"Blanton walked towards us. 'Yeah, Frog, whaddya ya want?'

'This is Fump. You got money?' Blanton nodded that he did.

'Well, you give Fump a cow and a calf [a hundred and fifty dollars] and I'll cover it.'

"Blanton reached into his watch pocket and pulled out a roll of fifty dollar bills, peeled off three, and handed them to me."[24]

Blanton's musical career was probably the shortest of all the important musicians in jazz history. In 1941, Ben was told not to share a hotel room with the young bass player anymore because he suffered from tuberculosis. "I got really mad and I said, 'How dare you tell me such filthy lies.' But when Ellington himself told me as well, I had to believe it."[25] Blanton was permanently replaced by Junior Raglin at the end of that year. Ellington did all he could. "I called doctor after doctor until I found out who the top people on TB were in Los Angeles. I made a date and took him down to the big city hospital... He hadn't been there two days when some cat went down and said to him, 'Why the idea of Duke leaving you here in the ward!' He packed him up and took him out somewhere near Pasadena, somewhere along a railroad siding.

"When I got back to town, there he was, on his cot. They had nothing there, no X-rays or anything. 'Well, you can't move him,' they said, and he should have been moved a month before I got there."[26]

Bass player Red Callender, who died early in 1992, had visited his sick colleague regularly. He believed that Blanton's friendship with Webster had contributed to his illness. "When you play bass with a big band you might have to change shirts or undershirts a few times a night, you perspire so much. This is how Blanton first contracted TB—improper care. Working in Chicago or some northern city, being wringing wet from playing all night, then going out on the town with someone who drinks like Ben—you get wiped out. Blanton was very frail; I don't think he weighed more than 130 pounds."[27]

Jimmy Rowles' statement confirms this. "There weren't any bass amplifiers back then, so Jimmy plucked himself ragged. Sweating profusely after a night of playing, he'd walk out to get some fresh air during the breaks. In Seattle, with his coat hanging wide open. Even though it's freezing up there! That's a good way to catch pneumonia."

But Milt Hinton doubts he was so reckless as to simply emulate his buddy's drinking. "Blanton was a smart guy, even though he was just a kid. He didn't smoke and drink and he kept his money in his pocket, even when he and Ben did the town."[28]

When Ellington and his band left California, Webster asked Hinton to keep an eye on the young bassist.

Hinton recalled, "I made it a point of visiting whenever I could and we'd talk until he got too tired to go on. It was a sad situation. He was just a kid, twenty-three or twenty-four, and completely alone out there."[29]

"Every night we played a radio broadcast, Chu Berry and I wrote him a song, which we played for the radio and dedicated to him. Afterward, we went to visit him—he had a radio next to his bed—and he'd start tellng us all kinds of things about chords. 'Hey, you're using a D flat ninth there, but you should have used *that* particular chord.' "[30]

On July 29, 1942, in the City of Hope Hospital in Los Angeles, he got a visit from Callender and Lee Young, Lester's brother, who played the drums. They found Blanton in his bed, emaciated. He was picking some strings on his guitar to keep his fingers in shape, and was too far gone to understand what was happening to him. He died the next day, at just 23 years and nine months of age.

Years later, one night in 1968, Webster rang Michiel de Ruyter's doorbell after a tour in Amsterdam. He was crying, and looked like he'd been sleeping in his clothes for a week. It took a while before he was able to say what the matter was: "*Blanton died.*"

※

The Duke knew how to make his performers give their all, but he was also not averse to borrowing their ideas. His new tenor player noticed this right away. It wasn't unusual for the piano chords to stop during solos while the chief got busy writing down some new idea he'd just heard.

Before Webster joined, Ellington had been used to writing for four saxes, so in the first months not all songs had a part for the new sax player. Ben was often left trying to find his own part. While he was fiddling around, Ellington kept some music paper handy to write down the new notes. According to Ellington's son Mercer, "Every time Ben got up and played by ear, the whole gang jumped on him and said, 'Hey, you've got my note!' So Ben decided he would get away from this and find a note nobody had... A semi-dissonant sound resulted from the five parts because there was no written part for him. Ellington heard it, liked it, and learned how to apply it."[31] However, those dissonants were more or less in Ellington's head already. After all, Webster had been amazed at the advanced sounds when he first joined, and Tizol had to reassure him that Ellington wanted it that way.

The sax player later called Ellington "the smartest thief," and rightly so. Although Webster wrote both the theme and sax chorus for "Cotton Tail," his boss inscribed himself as the song's composer and arranger. The song "Deary," composed by Webster, is included note for note in the "Brown" segment of Ellington's 1943 *Black, Brown and Beige Suite*. In 1942 or maybe '41, Webster recorded this song with a primitive recorder, singing to his own piano accompaniment.[32] It is almost redundant to add that Webster never collected any royalties for this.

The suite premiered in a benefit for Russian war veterans in Carnegie Hall on January 23, 1943. The orchestra was in great shape, but Ben, significantly, was not accorded a significant role. Out of the twenty-two pieces, and the suite—which lasted more than forty-five minutes—he was only given three solos. And the longest—on "Cotton Tail," of course—was spoiled when his employer kicked off a tempo that was much too fast to do it justice.[33] As a matter of fact, no noteworthy solos were produced during Webster's last six months with Ellington. Apparently, he was being shown the door. Ellington never fired anyone officially. He just made their life miserable, so they could plan an exit and eventually leave of their own accord.

Webster left the orchestra in August 1943 and wasn't properly replaced until 1950, when Paul Gonsalves joined. And why did he leave his favorite band? He had made such a name for himself as a soloist that he realized he could make more money and gain more notoriety by fronting an outfit himself. But there were additional factors, including alcohol, of course. Ben didn't drink as much as he would later on, and as a young man handled his liquor better, but he already drank enough for it to be an occasional nuisance. And on nights when things got a little free-form—at dance parties, for instance—he'd sometimes sit down behind the piano. Ellington didn't mind, but by the time the boss wanted to start playing again, Webster just wouldn't give way.

The United States' entry into the Second World War certainly upset the band's routine. They could no longer afford a luxury private train. Up to then, the band had

had two Pullmans: one reserved for the instruments, the other for eating and sleeping. This was especially convenient in the segregated South because it guaranteed the black band a place to rest and dine. The Ellingtonians—along with many another black orchestra—had to manage without this convenience after Pearl Harbor. Buses were confiscated by the army as well. Gas was rationed, and car tires were almost impossible to obtain. Sometimes, the musicians couldn't even secure a place on the public trains, and were forced to sit on their instrument case in the aisle the whole way. It appears that Bigard left the orchestra for just this reason. Tenor player Arnett Cobb, who worked with Lionel Hampton at the time: "Trains were always jam-packed in those days. That's when I learned to sleep standing up. You had to—sometimes there wasn't even enough room to sit on the floor."

Webster's last recordings with Ellington in this period date from August 1943. That same month, Ben went on to play with his own combo in The Three Deuces in New York, on legendary 52nd Street. According to Hinton, the owner of the club had offered him twice the amount he made with Ellington. Hinton: "Money and fame were very important to him, so he decided to leave."[34]

Webster always denied that there were personal conflicts. "I left the orchestra because I didn't get enough opportunities as a soloist. Ellington had no reason to let me play more than the others, he gives everybody the same chances, but that just wasn't enough for someone of my temperament... There was no animosity between us, I can't stress that enough."[35]

During his Amsterdam years, he talked about the *Black, Brown and Beige Suite* without a hint of resentment. Ben told Michiel de Ruyter that he and his drinking buddies in the band—trombonist Joe ("Tricky Sam") Nanton and trumpeter Rex Stewart—had been so taken with the composition that they didn't drink a drop during the rehearsals and performance.

※

During his Ellington period, Webster was briefly married to Doreen Williams (nickname Eudora). He met her through Clara Lewis (1918–1973), one of his second cousin Joyce's daughters. Ben and Clara—who played the piano—worked together in Washington D.C for a short while in the thirties.

It was hardly a storybook romance. Cohabitation was unheard of in those days, so it was common to get married to someone after only a brief courtship. A lot of these marriages foundered soon afterward because the spouses simply hadn't had much of a chance to get acquainted.

Ben and Eudora were married in Washington in 1941. They moved to a house in Los Angeles, in the area around Central Avenue. Shortly afterward, the orchestra went on another tour. The couple didn't have any children, and he apparently never fathered children with any other woman either.

Joyce: "He discovered that she had become involved with another musician while he was on tour. Now his mother was a very decent kind of woman, and he thought he would get the same type of woman when he got married. And when he discovered that she was not that type, he became outrageous and brutal. He beat her, because he just couldn't take it."[36]

The fights can't have been too severe, because Eudora and her new husband actually visited Ben in Amsterdam in the late sixties. Producer Johan van der Keuken recalled: "They were plain, middle-class people in their fifties. The guy worked for a bank. I met them once, because they went along when Ben had to play somewhere.

"That night Ben remarked, 'That man is a good provider.' By which he meant to say that he put bread on the table, but that there was nothing else remarkable about the man. He just didn't find him very interesting. Ben never talked about his marriage—that woman had simply been there, and then things went wrong."

In the late seventies, when a record was issued with some club recordings, she tried to claim some of the proceeds as Webster's widow—which was quite unreasonable, because at the time of Webster's death they had been separated for over thirty years. The album cover acknowledges that the publication had been made possible thanks to an arrangement with "Mrs. Eudora Webster, widow of the late Benjamin Francis Webster."[37] She died in the 1980s.

All this trouble was far away when a primitive cardboard record was made in 1941, with Eudora in a mock conversation. The recording was made without Webster's knowledge; the occasion was their imminent wedding.[38]

Unknown friend (trying to sound serious): "Miss Williams, in your opinion, who has the nicest tone of all sax players?"

Eudora: "Lester Young!"

Friend: "Yeah yeah, but what do you think about Ben Webster?"

E: "Who is that?"

F: "That is the man you're going to marry."

E: "Oh."

F: "And what about speed and virtuosity?"

E: "Eh... Tex Beneke. His technique is sooo impressive."

F: "Yes, but what about Ben Webster?"

E: "Who is Ben Webster?"

F: "That's the man you are going to marry."

E: "Ooooh..."

And so forth.

notes

1 *Down Beat*, June 26, 1958.

2 Duke Ellington, *The Blanton/Webster Band* (RCA Blue Bird 56592-RB—3 CD set). These contain all the essential studio recordings Webster made with with Ellington.

3 See note 2.

4 See note 2.

5 See note 2. "Mobile Bay," "Lament for Javanette," and the most important recordings of Ellington sidemen with Ben Webster can be found on *The Great Ellington Units*, RCA Blue Bird.

6 *Down Beat*, June 26, 1958.

7 *Music and Rhythm*, August 1941.

8 From the movie *Big Ben*, by Johan van der Keuken (1967).

9 See note 8.

10 Stanley Dance, *The World of Duke Ellington* (Charles Schribner's Sons 1970/1981).
11 See note 10.
12 See note 10.
13 *Melody Maker*, May 8, 1971.
14 See note 8.
15 See note 8.
16 Duke Ellington 1940, *Live From the Crystal Ballroom in Fargo, N.D., vol. 1* and *vol. 2*, Tax.
17 See note 10.
18 *Down Beat*, November 27, 1958.
19 *Jazz Nu*, March 1991.
20 See note 8.
21 See note 2.
22 See note 8.
23 Ira Gitler, *Swing to Bop* (Oxford University Press 1985).
24 Milt Hinton and David G. Berger, *Bass Line* (Temple University Press 1973).
25 See note 8.
26 Duke Ellington, *Music Is My Mistress* (Doubleday/Da Capo Press 1973).
27 Red Callender, *Unfinished Dream* (Quartet Books 1985).
28 Milt Hinton and David G. Berger, *Bass Line* (Temple University Press 1988).
29 See note 28.
30 See note 28.
31 See note 10.
32 Never released on record.
33 Duke Ellington: *The Carnegie Hall Concert*, Prestige.
34 See note 28.
35 *Jazz Magazine*, May 1965.
36 From the movie *The Brute and the Beautiful*, by John Jeremy (1989).
37 *At The Nuway Club*, Jazz Guild.
38 Never released on record.

52nd st. —on his own

Everybody played with everybody else on 52nd Street, the mecca for jazz fans and musicians in the first half of the forties. The artists all worked with their own combos, but could be found jamming with other artists half the time. The musicians' union didn't yet have a problem with this, and club owners liked anything that kept the beer tap flowing.

Drummer Shelly Manne: "The pay wasn't good. But anytime I had a choice between working a club gig somewhere or working on The Street, I'd grab the 52nd St. job, no matter how much loot I had to give up. Those years, from '39 to '46, were the liveliest of my life and the most formative."[1]

It's easy to imagine how little money was to be made when you consider that The Three Deuces, where both Art Tatum and Ben Webster's groups worked in the second half of 1943, was no more than a long, narrow basement furnished with three rows of tables. That fall, the Onyx across the street featured nightly entertainment by Billie Holiday and guitarist Al Casey's trio,

Webster in 1944

alternating nightly with a formation led by Dizzy Gillespie and Oscar Pettiford.

Ben Webster was a familiar figure in New York when he started working in The Three Deuces in 1943. He had been one of Ellington's main solo players for over three and a half years. His ballads were admired by one and all, and young tenor players would learn his "Cotton Tail" choruses by heart. When he was in town with the orchestra, he'd often go out jamming in clubs.

Milt Hinton: "I remember one particular session. Ben Webster and Prez [Lester Young] were there and everybody knew about it... Each had his individual rhythm section to play for him. A drummer and I played for Ben. Walter Page and Jo Jones played for Prez. The room was filled with smoke and loaded with musicians."[2] In 1941 and 1942 he took part in the Sunday afternoon jam sessions at Kelly's Stable. These sessions were organized by Teddy Reig, who later went on to become a record producer. Reig: "At one of our sessions we had both Ben Webster and Coleman Hawkins. Ben had just come back from California with Duke and was pretty hot with "Just A-Settin' and A-Rockin' " and "Cotton Tail." He told me, 'I want Hawk!' I said, 'Okay, we'll get you Hawk.' I begged Hawkins to do it and he agreed, but for $20 which was double what we usually paid.

"Sunday came, and Ben went up to the mike, all big, bad and bold. He growled out a chorus and Hawk egged him on, saying 'C'mon, take some more.' Ben looked at him a little suspiciously but went ahead. And then Hawk took over where he left off and buried him. When we looked around, there was no more Ben Webster. He didn't even finish the set, never mind the gig. That night, we were back at Minton's, lining up the acts for next week, when in walks Ben, completely crocked. He's waving a clarinet in his hand, yelling, 'Get me Barney Bigard!' "[3]

The most famous jam session club—Minton's Playhouse—was not on 52nd Street, but in Harlem. Almost all young, hip musicians went over there at night. For revolutionaries like Dizzy Gillespie, Thelonious Monk, and Charlie Christian, it was a kind of home away from home. Yet another gathering place for young musicians was Monroe's Uptown House, which moved to the Street in 1943, the year that Charlie Parker had a steady gig there. Parker played the tenor back then; Earl Hines' big band, where he also had a contract, already had two altos when he joined.

Parker's favorite song was "Cherokee," which he played at hyperventilation speed. According to legend, Webster pulled the sax out of his mouth on the night they first met, and told him, "You shouldn't be playing so fast on that thing!" But after he had gotten over his initial surprise, Webster told anyone who would listen that there was a new sax player in town, and everybody should prepare to be amazed.

Webster mostly preferred Minton's, the club where—as everybody knows—bebop was born. Did he like this new music? Stories about this conflict. Budd Johnson described Lester Young and Ben's visits to Minton's as follows: "As I remember, once Prez walked into

Minton's, and Ben, and they were gonna jam with the group. Of course the guys tested them out, their knowledge, and they started to play Monk's tunes, and they didn't know which way the tune was going because it was so different from anything they had played before. It was a lot of fun because the guys were anxious to learn—nobody put them down—and they were very happy to sit in and try to do this and catch these sounds."[4] To which Webster himself added, "Don Byas and Prez and I would make it up to Minton's every night just to play. Sometimes, sitting in can get to be a clambake. But those days, we were playing to really play."[5]

Bass player Gene Ramey told writer Stanley Dance a different story. "Prez, Ben Webster, and Roy Eldridge were the only people who were really vocal about the new rhythm sections... They played their solo in phrases, and when a guy dropped a bomb in the middle it killed the phrase. Prez would turn around and say, 'Just give me some tinkdee-doo...' They didn't like what was going on in the rhythm section, and they didn't like the flatted fifths and that stuff."[6]

Was Webster a conservative or a progressive? The truth lies somewhere in between. He was enough of a musician to see the value of the new direction, but disliked certain aspects of it. The earliest bebop sounded quite nervous and agitated—later on, the rougher edges got smoothed out. A good example of the process can be traced in Kenny Clarke's recordings: some of his earlier work sounds like detonation, but later on his style becomes much simpler. Bop calmed down a little, which made it acceptable to most musicians and music lovers—except of course to Dance, who remained a collector of anti-bebop testimonials up to his death in 1999.

Webster had no trouble playing together with the modernists. He liked going to Minton's, and Charlie Parker was part of his quintet as a second wind player at the Onyx for a while in 1945. Ben was not a typical bopper, of course, but he had a certain flexibility to his style. He was a supple player, who mainly focused on melodic play. When pianists played advanced chords he wouldn't follow them note for note, but he did play in such a way that harmony was preserved. A drummer was allowed to hit bebop accents, but only within limits.

"I listened to a lot of Charlie Parker back then... I'd never heard anybody play so many chords so fast, and all in the right place too." But little changed for Webster, because, "I've never had the aspiration to be a fast sax player."[7] He also noted, "It's one thing to keep up with modern trends, but to go all out for it body and soul when your own background is different is something else again." In the same interview, he praised Stan Getz "for his technique, his ideas, and his beautiful tone," and Sonny Stitt, "who is very underrated."[8]

His problem wasn't so much the changing music as the level of his fellow players. Milt Hinton: "In Duke's band he was used to playing with a high-caliber rhythm section—Sonny Greer, Jimmie Blanton, and Duke himself. But on 52nd Street things were very different. An owner might give a star a high salary but there was never enough left to pay for a good rhythm section. So, like so many other guys who went out on their own, Ben often worked with second-rate sidemen...

"At first he'd spend set after set showing them what he wanted, but after a while he realized it was hopeless. He'd even complain to the boss about the problem, but the answer was always the same: 'Whadya want from me? I got a budget for music and most of it goes to pay you...'

"Booze was always a big part of the jazz club scene. Back then, things got so frustrating for Ben, that the only way he could cope was to get loaded every night."[9]

Shortly after the start of the engagement at The Three Deuces, Webster asked Billy Taylor to replace the mediocre pianist who had first been hired. He had met Taylor at Minton's, the place where the 22-year-old went the very night he moved to New York (he was originally from Washington, D.C.). Taylor was quite a good pianist but was young and still unknown in New York, which made him cheap. (He should not be confused with the bass player of the same name who was Blanton's predecessor in Ellington's band.)

Besides Ben himself and Taylor, Webster's group consisted of the excellent, versatile drummer Specs Powell and two relatively obscure figures, guitar player Teddy Walters and bass player Charlie Drayton. Powell left after a while—likely because of the poor pay—and went on to work as a CBS studio musician. He was replaced by Jimmy Crawford, the former Jimmy Lunceford percussionist.

Ben had been playing at The Three Deuces for just over

two months when the first bebop combo was booked, in the Onyx on the other side of The Street. This was a quartet consisting of Dizzy Gillespie, Oscar Pettiford playing bass, Max Roach on drums, and, on tenor, first Lester Young, later Don Byas.[10]

The pianist was supposed to have been Bud Powell, but he was already employed in Cootie Williams' big band. Williams was his legal guardian as well, and refused to let him leave. As Powell was underage, he had no choice but to comply. The group initially performed as a quartet without a pianist for that reason.

Taylor was drawn to the progressive sounds of Dizzy's combo, so he offered to play with the boppers for free, between his sets in The Three Deuces. The inevitable happened: he kept sticking around with Dizzy's group, and ended up being late for his real job more and more often. Three Deuces owner Irving Alexander eventually got fed up and fired him. Incidentally, it was not Taylor who was eventually hired at the Onyx, but George Wallington.

※

Webster usually waited until after his job at The Three Deuces before he went jamming. Between sets, he'd usually hang out at The White Rose, where whiskey cost only 35 cents, and other drinks were a quarter. The place was always packed with musicians. Whenever young musicians like Billy Taylor or Shelly Manne dared order a beer, he'd yell to the bartender, "Give this kid a coke and nothing stronger!"

It is not certain who became Webster's next pianist, but

he must have gone through a lot of trouble to replace Taylor. He knew plenty of good players in New York, of course. One of the pianists he was still in contact with was Clyde Hart, a musician with an ear for new jazz. Webster contracted him for a few record sessions, but he was too expensive for club work.

Hart wasn't doing very well when they met again on 52nd street. He had spent time in the hospital for tuberculosis. He had hated the place so much that he'd run away, and refused to be recommitted. Hart's wife Edna, Webster, trombone player Trummy Young and Budd Johnson tried to take care of him, but to no avail. He died on March 19, 1945, at age 34 or 35.

According to trumpet player and jazz writer Rex Stewart—generally a reliable source—during his 52nd Street period Ben once showed his good heart by saving a woman's life. "I well remember hearing of an incident that took place just about that time. I heard it from one of Ben's boon companions, a fellow whom I knew only as Slim. He told me that early one morning, while they were getting the air in Slim's car, on Harlem River Drive, a young woman jumped into the river. Ben yelled to Slim to stop the car, and as soon as he did, Ben dived in, clothes and all, and saved her. Ben is modest; he even denies remembering this incident."[11]

In the fall of 1944, Webster played in the Downbeat Club in Chicago for a few months. This club also employed a trio managed by the 25-year-old pianist Argonne Thornton. After a few gigs and a series of radio broadcasts together, Webster took the trio back to the Onyx in

New York with him. Thornton—who changed his name to Sadik Hakim after his conversion to Islam in 1947—was Ben's pianist for 15 months, until the end of 1945.

Thornton was a moderately good soloist back then, and a passable accompanist. Every Parker fan knows him because he was in the record studio with Parker on November 26, 1945 for a session that produced some world-famous recordings—although Thornton's solos are mostly stumbling, downward chromatic runs. According to most sources he was a pleasant young man eager to learn, who gladly suffered Webster's drinking. Webster liked him a lot, and on several occasions protected him against racist soldiers from the South (who were plentiful on The Street during the war years). One time, Thornton was threatened with a knife. Webster was at the other end of the Onyx at the time, and a room jammed full of tables separated him from the scene. He moved toward the fight like a steam roller, pushing aside tables without even thinking about it. He grabbed the southerner by the neck and held him a foot off the ground for a while, meanwhile reassuring his pianist. The redneck was trying to squirm out of his grip with all his might, and seemed to be at the point of suffocation when Webster finally opened his hand. He dropped down hard, and got out as fast as his feet could carry him.

During the period with Thornton, the group played almost exclusively in the Onyx, usually with forgotten sidemen like bassists Leo Guarnieri and Raele Wilson, and drummer Hillyard Brown.

In early 1945, Webster decided to be a little less frugal and hire a good second wind player. This turned the quartet into a quintet. His player of choice was Charlie Parker, but he wasn't going to stick around either. As soon as a set was over, Parker ran across the street to the Deuces where Dizzy was playing. He was usually still playing there when Ben returned from The White Rose after the intermission. "Then I'd go to the Deuces, where Parker was playing all these weird changes with Dizzy, and I'd shout to him, 'You're making your money over there, in the Onyx, not in here!' "[12]

According to Thornton, "Bird was never on time for work. One night he came in with his sax hidden under his coat, and he started playing as soon as he walked in the front door. He walked right up to the stage before we had any idea where the sounds were coming from."[13]

There were times when Ben didn't have such a hard time with his musicians on 52nd Street. In June and July of 1944, he was a guest player with the John Kirby Sextet. Judging from some live recordings that were issued later on, he had no difficulty adjusting to their style.[14]

In the first half of 1944, he played in The Three Deuces for a time as part of a renowned quartet led by one of the Street's best and most flexible drummers, 'Big Sid' Sidney Catlett. In mid '44, Catlett was offered a gig in California. Webster was sick on the day they departed, so at Catlett's request the 18-year-old Zoot Sims—an admirer of both Webster and Lester Young—took his place. This was the end of that quartet, although

Webster and Cartlett ended up playing together in different formations later on.

The 'Sid Catlett Quartet Featuring Ben Webster' was one of the few groups Ben played with in the studio as well as in clubs during those years; in March of 1944, the quartet recorded seven pieces in two days. The rhythm section is a relief after listening to almost all of Webster's earlier recordings.[15]

An even better recording is the one he made earlier that month with yet another versatile drummer, Cozy Cole. The accompaniment consisted of nimble Johnny Guarnieri on piano, Teddy Walters on guitar, and the former Ellington bass player Billy Taylor, and they possessed a Basie-like suppleness. Webster was invariably in top form, and produced a singular interpretation of "Body and Soul." After a sultry start with a lot of breath mixed in with the notes, he switched to a faster tempo and tore through the chord sequence with great energy.[16]

In a different session, neither the accompanying players nor the soloist were in as good form. The session, led by Webster, with Clyde Hart and drummer Denzil Best, was recorded in March '44.[17] He made several much better recordings with reed player Walter Thomas in 1944 and 1945, with good tenor solos on slow numbers like "Blues on the Bayou" and "Blues on the Delta," and on a composition depressingly titled "The Bottle is Empty."[18] On April 17, 1944 Webster—this time as leader—recorded four excellent pieces in which Hawkins' influence again asserts itself.[19]

⁂

After leaving Ellington's orchestra in August of 1943 Webster played almost exclusively with small formations, but there were exceptions. In 1948 and 1949 he performed with Ellington again—this will be discussed later. In the fall of 1943 he sat in with Count Basie, an ex-colleague from the Bennie Moten band. Don Byas, one of Basie's tenorists at the time, hadn't shown up yet, so Webster picked up his sax and took his place for the time being. This resulted in Byas losing his job; in Basie tenorist Buddy Tate's words, "Ben Webster came down one night when we were at the Hotel Lincoln, and he sat in Don's chair and played. I never heard anyone sound like that in my life, and all the cats flipped over Ben. Poor Don went across the street and got stoned!"[20] The incident started a rivalry between Webster and Byas that persisted through his Dutch years.

Because many musicians were being drafted for the war, a lot of big bands had a difficult time finding musicians. In 1943 and '44, Woody Herman had such trouble hiring top soloists that he hired some Ellington musicians for a number of record sessions, including Hodges, Tizol, and Ellington veteran Webster. The tenor solos on these recordings are not especially noteworthy. Ben does a professional job, but doesn't go all-out.[21]

More significant are some 1944 recordings under the direction of Georgie Auld, a then 24-year-old tenor player who, in a reckless mood, had both Webster and Hawkins come to the studio. Webster, trying to outdo the other, carries on with terrific speed through the quick blues of "Pick Up Boys," a speed never quite surpassed by even the heaviest tenor players.[22]

The young clarinet player Tony Scott asked him for a record session as well, which yielded a beautiful solo on the old Ellington hit "All Too Soon," with the melody sung by Sarah Vaughan.[23] Webster also played a charming bit part in recordings directed by Teddy Wilson and Benny Morton in 1945.[24]

Ben himself led two sessions in 1946 with Sid Catlett and guitar player Bill De Arango. These recordings show once again that Ben invested more physical energy in his solos back then, before his play took on a more pensive, contemplative character. In "I Got It Bad," you can hear that he still doesn't allow himself sufficient space in a lot of places, and that he is afraid to incorporate enough pauses to bring his ballads to a successful close. Other than that, his style is well on the way to being perfected. The solo on "Frog and Mule," for instance, could just as easily have been played twenty years later, in the exact same way.[25]

※

From the end of 1946 on, 52nd Street began losing its attraction, for various reasons. The Street was gaining a reputation as a cesspool of drink, drugs, prostitution, and crime, and attracted a lot of journalists looking for sensational stories. Resident homeowners saw the value of their real estate decline, and did little to promote the jazz climate. Police would raid the street on a regular basis, and on the slightest pretext.

The customers were starting to complain about the

expensive drinks and uncomfortable clubs, musicians about the meager pay. Teddy Reig remembered: "At Kelly's Stable...a bottle of beer was forty cents. They had a bartender named Harry who would try to grab away your bottle. You had to hold it with both hands. If you let go for a second, Harry would snatch it and say, 'Alright, what're you having?' And if you didn't order something, they'd throw you out."[26]

Club owners learned that you could make just as much money if you hired a stripper and a couple of third-rate musicians as accompaniment, and you wouldn't have to deal with these eccentric, conceited jazz musicians. The clubs where Webster's artistic triumphs took place either all closed or gave up jazz. Some new jazz clubs did open elsewhere in the city, but good gigs became harder to come by.

On February 24, 1950, *Down Beat* featured the headline, "The Street Has Become A Boring Alley Again." Webster was already gone by that time. He had done hardly any studio work in 1947 and 1948, and refused any longer to play with inferior musicians. In 1948, he decided to return to Ellington. In November he played along as a guest soloist, and he accompanied Duke on several tours afterward.

This brief, second Ellington period didn't yield any notable recordings for Webster enthusiasts. No significant new parts were written for Ben, but he did get to revisit earlier successes like "Cotton Tail" and "Just-A-Settin' and A-Rockin'." He played both of these at Carnegie Hall on November 13, 1948.[27] It was not just

Webster who was making few recordings; there was a recording ban in effect in 1948 and 1949. Because of a conflict about fees between the union and the record companies, almost the entire record business was put on hold during this period.

There are some surviving live recordings made in May 1949 with a group under Benny Carter's direction. Ben played the lead part on four pieces, and captivated the audience with his forceful yet sophisticated play. After the first few notes of the "Cotton Tail" theme, the audience started cheering as though he was a popular singer introducing a recent hit song.[28]

Webster only stayed with the orchestra until the summer of 1949, probably because of the strained relations between him and Ellington, and because of his own need for independence. It's clear that the boss hadn't counted on a long stay, because he had never relieved his regular tenor players, Al Sears and Charlie Rouse. For a short while, the orchestra contained as many as six reeds. When Webster had had enough of New York and Ellington he returned to Kansas City—to Mayme and Mom.

notes

1 Arnold Shaw, *The Street That Never Slept* (Coward, McCann & Geoghehan 1971). Later released as *52nd Street/The Street of Jazz* (Da Capo 1988).

2 Nat Shapiro and Nat Hentoff (edd.), *Hear Me Talkin' to Ya* (Penguin Books 1955/1966).

3 Teddy Reig and Edward Berger, *Reminiscing in Tempo* (Scarecrow Press and the Institute of Jazz Studies 1990).

4 Ira Gitler, *Swing to Bop* (Oxford University Press 1985).

5 *Down Beat*, June 26, 1958.

6 Stanley Dance, *The World of Count Basie* (Charles Schribner's Sons 1980).

7 Bery Vuijsje, *Jazzportretten* (Van Gennep 1983).

8 *Down Beat*, October 5, 1955.

9 Milt Hinton and David G. Berger, *Bass Line* (Temple University Press 1988).

10 The order in which the two tenors played in this group is mistakenly reversed in most books.

11 Rex Stewart, *Jazzmasters of the 30's* (Macmillan Publishing Co., a collection of articles from the 1960s).

12 See note 7.

13 Rob Reisner, *Bird: The Legend of Charlie Parker* (Quartet Books 1962).

14 *A Tribute To a Great Jazzman*, Archives of Jazz.

15 *Sid Catlett 1944–1946*, Classics.

16 Various artists: *The Savoy Sessions*, Savoy.

17 *Ben and the Boys*, Jazz Archives.

18 *The Walter "Foots" Thomas All Stars*, Prestige/Bellaphon.

19 *The Savoy Session/The Tenor Sax album*, Savoy.

20 Stanley Dance, *The World Of Count Basie* (Charles Schribner's Sons 1980).

21 Woody Herman: *Pre-Herds*, Affinity.

22 Coleman Hawkins, *Rainbow Mist*, Delmark.

23 *52nd Street, vol. 1* Polydor/Onyx Records Select 2344 049 (LP).

24 *Teddy Wilson 1942–1945*, Classics. The recordings with Morton were later issued under Barney Bigard's name as *Barney's Bounce*, Two Flats Disc 5002 (LP).

25 Coleman Hawkins/Ben Webster/Julian Dash: *Sax, vol. 1*, Doctor Jazz (CD).

26 Teddy Reig and Edward Berger, *Reminiscing in Tempo* (Scarecrow Press and the Institute of Jazz Studies 1990).

27 Duke Ellington, *The Carnegie Hall Concert*, Prestige.

28 Various Artists: *Big Sound Tenors*, Riverboat (LP).

norman granz and the fruitful fifties

Tenor sax player Harold Ashby: "Ben came back to Kansas City because his mother and his grandmother [*sic*] lived there. He hadn't been there for a couple of years. He worked in the Parkview Hotel. They had a nightclub there. All the pimps and gamblers gathered there—everybody. I was standing at the bar one time while Ben was playing a solo. One of his ballads. And there was this girl, you know, one top-notch girl. A fellow bought her drinks and offered her about a hundred dollars while Ben played his solo. And she said: 'No, no, not right now, I want to listen to the band.' And he said: 'Hundred dollars, baby.' A hundred dollars to turn the trick, that was a whole lot of money in 1949. But she refused. She just stood there and listened to the band. The cash register was silent, everything stopped. That's how Ben played."[1]

⁂

In the fifties, when Webster was in his 40s, his style reached full maturity. The restlessness that had sometimes marred his earlier solos became a thing of the past. Complex chord transitions were managed in a smooth and subtle way. A good demonstration of this is "Chelsea Bridge," one of his favorite ballads. With Ellington he played it in a medium dance tempo, but now he was able to slow the tempo considerably and caress the melody.[2]

In his rendition it sounds like a pretty simple piece, but one look at the chord scheme proves otherwise. This Billy Strayhorn composition contained harmonies that were very unusual for the time—but it is typical of Webster not to impose these on his audience. He no longer needed to play the smart guy, and instead drapes the melody over the chords with a seeming simplicity that offsets the harmonies. He began playing more and more sparingly and sensually. The increasing availability of good microphones also enabled him to blow more gently, and enhanced the effect of mixing his breath in with the music. Soloists like him are rare now. Current avant-gardists favor irony, intellectual games, and commenting on other music. These elements are absent from Webster's work. He doesn't want to confuse the listener, but pampers them instead with soft, comforting sounds. He takes you to bed, tucks you in, and asks if you want the light in the hallway left on. His music comes straight from the heart, without any detours.

Whitney Balliett described it this way: "His style is easy, magisterial, and enveloping; it *embraces* the listener. Many jazz musicians, through timidity, lack of technique, or plain blurriness, make the listener do much of the work; Webster, an old family retainer, meets his audience three-quarters of the way."[3]

※

In Kansas City, it was like Ben had returned to square one. He was back in his hometown after his marriage failed, he hadn't been able to stay with Ellington, and could no longer find work in New York. So now he was back to playing the blues with local musicians. Life was slower-paced out there, and he had no trouble finding simple gigs, but the musicians he played with were often of a lower caliber than their New York counterparts.

When you listen to two sessions with Jay McShann in Kansas City—one with singer Walter Brown, one under Shann's name—it seems like time has stood still. The repertoire consists of all kinds of blues variations, and the rhythm sections play a rather stiff four beats to the measure. But Webster seems to be having a great time in this unpretentious company.[4]

※

In the fall of 1951, Mayme and Mom moved to Los Angeles. They had found a large white house on a leafy boulevard, in one of the city's better neighborhoods. Their son trailed along. He had friends in Kansas City and enjoyed a certain repute, but there wasn't much there for him otherwise. The Kansas City scene had really fallen apart thirteen years earlier when Pendergast was arrested. Los Angeles had many more clubs, and was also home to a lot of record companies and their studios.

He did indeed find work in L.A., although at first it was

not the kind of work he expected. In the fifties a lot of producers hired jazz musicians, and especially tenorists, as background players for popular artists. Budd Johnson, Al Sears, and Sam Taylor were all hired to anonymously play on all kinds of hit songs. These gigs were offered Webster as well. In December 1951, he appeared as the guest soloist on records by singer/vibraphone player Johnny Otis, blues singer/guitarist Pete "Guitar" Lewis, and singers Little Esther and Dorothy Ellis.[5]

The Otis recordings contain some fine dance music—with supportive roaring and tearing by Webster—and three memorable "Stardust" takes. Later on, he recorded a very soulful "Trouble In Mind" with singer Dinah Washington. He also made a very odd little record in December 1952 with vocal quartet The Ravens. It contains the lively "I'll Be Back" and the sultry "Don't Mention My Name." Jukebox music was still pretty jazzy in those days, so Webster didn't have to hold back in the least.[6]

On December 27, 1951, he made his first recordings as lead artist in four-and-a-half years, with Benny Carter and bass player John Kirby (who died six months later). They only recorded four sides, but the results are phenomenal. Webster's style had reached its prime, and he absolutely shines on "Old Folks" and "You're My Thrill."[7]

※

This session marked the beginning of a fruitful period, mainly because producer and concert organizer Norman Granz happened to be in L.A as well. Granz had a kind of placement agency for jazz stars, and he regularly got them all into the studio for concerts that felt like public jam sessions. These spectacles were known as *Jazz at the Philharmonic* (JATP) after the first large concert in the series, which took place on July 2, 1944 in the Los Angeles Philharmonic Auditorium.

Granz wasn't new to organizing jam session concerts. In June 1942, he had created some ad hoc combos for a series of Sunday afternoon sessions in the Trouville Club in Los Angeles. On one of these Sundays—June 28, to be precise—Webster shared the stage with Lester Young and Joe Thomas. *Down Beat* reported that "they were literally carving each other into strips."[8]

Granz's stable included Lester Young, Flip Phillips, and Illinois Jacquet (tenor); Tommy Turk and Bill Harris (trombone); Dizzy Gillespie, Roy Eldridge, and Charlie Shavers (trumpet); Willie Smith, Benny Carter, and Charlie Parker (alto); Buddy Rich, J.C. Heard, Louie Bellson, and Gene Krupa (drums); Oscar Peterson and Hank Jones (piano); Ray Brown (bass); Herb Ellis and Barney Kessel (guitar), and singer Ella Fitzgerald.

These musicians—and dozens of others—were the pool from which Granz recruited. He knew Webster from his work with Ellington, heard him play live a few times in L.A., and decided to add him to his team—which meant tours with the JATP players and a lot of record sessions for Granz' labels. This chapter will mostly be devoted to record reviews, simply because so many great records were produced during these years.

For Webster, a JATP night would usually entail several

Norman Granz

long solos over simple, harmonic chords—frequently the blues and the chords of "I Got Rhythm"—and a ballad medley. These concerts, recorded on a great number of records, unfortunately don't contain many remarkable Webster solos. During the ballad medleys he was able to go at his own speed, but in the higher tempos he did little more than hurry on louder and louder, with fewer and fewer notes, accompanied by a rhythm section that sounded like they were driving piles. Sometimes he'd hold one note for a while, with small variations—a trick invented by Lester Young, later popularized by Illinois Jacquet.

The result was exciting for the people in the auditorium, as is apparent from the enthusiastic cheers, but today it makes tedious listening. Webster could tear and squeak, but it was not his strong suit—especially when he had to keep it up for twenty choruses.

Fortunately, Granz provided pleasant working conditions. He organized well-paid tours in large, sold-out halls, in good musical company. This contributed to the popularity of jazz in general, and to that of his solo players in particular. Granz was both a businessman and a jazz fan—a rare combination. Just to give an idea of what this meant for his players: Lester Young earned $750 per week touring with JATP, while the famous Birdland club paid him no more than $125.

Critic Nat Hentoff wrote of Granz' work in the fifties: "It is Granz, incidentally, who has persisted in providing a forum for musicians like Roy, Ben Webster, and Lester Young, despite sales apathy among the newer generation of record buyers, most of whom seem to feel either that jazz grew from Stan Kenton's forehead or that anything after Duke Ellington is jazz-in-its-corrupted-decline."[9]

It is interesting to note that Granz didn't want to know about segregation. He let blacks and whites travel together, play together, and booked everyone into the same hotels. His reputation allowed him to do it—he simply refused to do business with anyone who objected.

It would go a bit too far to review all the JATP records here; the music isn't interesting enough for that. One typical JATP concert took place in Tokyo on November 18, 1953, as part of Webster's first tour outside North America. The players started off with a fast blues number, dubbed "Tokyo Blues" for the occasion. Webster took seventeen choruses, and after a brief preamble he launched into a rough-edged sound. This was followed by "Up," a feature for drummer J.C. Heard, where Webster had hardly any role at all.

"Cotton Tail" was repeated once more with Flip Phillips. Webster took eleven choruses, starting with his Ellington solo and followed by an uninspired growling that lasts a long time. He got a chance to make up for all this noise in the standard ballad medley. In this recording, he chose his usual "Someone To Watch Over Me."

He now had to wait in the dressing room while several sets were performed by smaller groups, led by Oscar Peterson, Gene Krupa, and Ella Fitzgerald, respectively. It wasn't until the Fitzgerald finale that he was allowed to briefly get on stage to add some noise. In short: out of the two-and-a-half-hour concert, Webster blows only four solos, of which only one is at his usual level.[10]

As soon as Granz moved the jam sessions to the studio, there was room for more nuance and creativity. Webster's first recording under Granz' supervision took place in July '52, with saxophonists Phillips, Parker, Hodges, and Carter. These recordings are a lot more musical (rather than just ostentatious), and the sound is a lot better than on the live recordings. It is always a pleasure to see Ray Brown's name on the cover, but it's even better to actually hear him play.[11] Ben's confidence increased once he had some nice offers from Granz in his pocket, so he moved back to New York in the fall of '52. He now started a stream of record sessions, mostly for Granz' Verve label, that lasted through the fifties.

He worked for other labels too; in 1953 he recorded three nice titles for EmArcy with an orchestra led by Johnny Richards.[12] But these non-Verve records are mostly not on the level of the Granz studio sessions. One exception is a live recording of some February 1953 concerts with the Modern Jazz Quartet. The gap between bebop and swing had diminished in those years, so Ben played along well with bop drummer Kenny Clarke featuring his own repertoire—"Danny Boy," "Poutin'," "Cotton Tail," etc.—as well as the Parker themes "Billie's Bounce" and "Confirmation."[13] Stanley Dance was effectively refuted...

Webster's first masterpiece for Verve, *King of the Tenors*, was recorded in May and December of 1953. This is truly a historic recording, which each and every jazz fan should have in their collection. This was the first long-playing record by the 'ripe' tenor, recorded in stereo. The accompaniment is top of the mark: Oscar Peterson—who on other dates produces too many notes—shows uncommon restraint, and combines forces with bass player Ray Brown and drummer J.C. Heard to provide an ideal background for Webster.[14]

Webster's ears had become sensitive after working with Hinton and Blanton, so he got along well with Ray Brown. "You could float on those bass notes, you hardly had to play at all for it to sound good," he told Michiel de Ruyter fifteen years later. Throughout the fifties, he reached several additional heights with Peterson's trio.

The rhythm section is like a group of ideal butlers—the gentlemen politely remain in the background, but as soon as you need them, they're right there. These are the same musicians that played in the wild JATP sessions, but they sound more at home here. Webster's play is characterized by a noble simplicity. In the ballads "Tenderly," "That's All," and "Danny Boy" he does little more than play the melody, with small variations. The tenor sound has been recorded very prominently, and envelops the listener like a woolen blanket. "Cotton Tail" is repeated once more as well, but this time Webster gets to set the tempo, so it's not played at the usual breakneck speed.

The ballad "Danny Boy" becomes a compelling tear-jerker, especially in the second chorus, which Webster opens an octave higher, in the alto register. In his study

The Swing Era, Gunther Schuller nominates this solo one of "Webster's all-time sublime performances," and characterizes the second chorus as "another subtle tribute to Hodges."[15]

In 1954 and '55, four sessions with ballads only followed. The first, on March 30, 1954, included a beautiful version of "My Funny Valentine." It also featured "Sophisticated Lady" with Teddy Wilson, and two lesser known songs, "You're Mine" and "Love's Away." He sticks close to the melody again, but grabs people's attention through small accent shifts and all kinds of tonal variation; he'll let a note crescendo to full volume and then fade away, or sneak up on it from below.

In the other three sessions he is backed by a string orchestra, which makes for less interesting results. Webster's play, normally just shy of the sentimental, benefited most from a simple setting. The string players are as superfluous here as salt on an anchovy pizza, or sugar on a birthday cake. The tenor player puts more than enough velvet, romance, and moonlight into his music without them. And as soon as the orchestra starts playing more prominently, they interrupt the tenor solos rather than support them. The limited repertoire doesn't encourage Webster's creativity either; just as on stage, he needed regular tempo changes to keep his inspiration up.[16]

※

In 1956 he moved back to Los Angeles, where he remained until the fall of '57. Again, he hadn't been able to get as much work as he had hoped in the New York clubs. Managing his own engagements proved difficult, and competition was stiff. New trends like hardbop and cool jazz were the talk of the day, and magazines preferred to write about big name tenor saxophonists like Coleman Hawkins and Lester Young, soon followed by Sonny Rollins and John Coltrane. His main sources of income were Granz' record sessions and the JATP tours—so why hang around New York? He didn't need a New York base for his JATP trips, and L.A. had plenty of studios, as well as the added attraction of being able to stay with Mayme and Mom, in a warmer climate.

On the West Coast, the studio work continued at the same fast clip. Two sessions with Billie Holiday in August 1956 contained some appropriate songs—he inserts a few enormous sighs into "Ill Wind," "Do Nothin' 'til You Hear From Me," and "Sophisticated Lady."[17] At four subsequent Holiday sessions—all in January 1957—he was asked to sit in again.[18] These recordings also yielded good results, though the singer's voice had certainly suffered some erosion by that time. Webster's soft, supporting obligatos are never in Holiday's way—he mostly inserts his melodies where Holiday pauses. And his dark, velvety sound never enters her register. His quietly humming notes sound like a gently concurring, sympathetic mumble, especially when the singer bemoans another unhappy love affair: "That's it Billie, you're right, they're all jerks."

※

In Los Angeles, he met up with Art Tatum again, the pianist he most revered. Granz was having Art play with as many important mainstream soloists as possible, and now that Webster was in the neighborhood, he too got to make a record with the piano giant. Ben later repeatedly said he considered this his best album. His fans almost always disagree.

Tatum was a true virtuoso on the piano, but not a very good accompanist. His right hand keeps hammering out fast phrases, even when Webster is supposed to be soloing. Oscar Peterson was better able to restrain himself when performing as an accompanist. He would also insert short breaks for Ray Brown to fill with riffs. Tatum plays all these bass riffs himself with his left hand, leaving Red Callender with little to add. Drummer Bill Douglas gets to act as a rhythm box, and Webster doesn't manage to get beyond some tentative humming.[19]

Why was Webster so taken with this record? A self-taught musician from Kansas City, he greatly admired Tatum, who could play all sorts of classical pieces backwards, and had extensive knowledge of harmony and technique. Because of his admiration, he failed to realize that their talents weren't all that compatible. According to trumpet player Harry Edison, he nevertheless had the guts once to tell Tatum off: "He was playing a beautiful solo on this date. But Art, he wasn't quite an accompanist, he was a soloist. And he was playing so much through Ben's solo that Ben stopped the record and said: 'This is my solo Art, and not yours. And I would appreciate it if you would just play some accompaniment and not play through my solo.' And everybody laughed, 'cause who dared to say a thing like that to Art Tatum?"[20]

Still, Webster was of the opinion that the piano virtuoso was restraining himself, compared to other occasions. "He really accompanied me. I believe that was a sign that he appreciated my playing, because I know certain records with other musicians where he just played on, from the beginning of a piece all the way to the end."[21]

Ten years later, when asked to name the pianists he most admired, he said, "Hank Jones, George Shearing, Oscar Peterson, and Teddy Wilson are good pianists, but you just cannot compare them with Tatum. As for the young kids: Bill Evans makes nice music... Norman Granz deserves the respect of the entire jazz world, because he gave Tatum the opportunity to make records where, when, and with whomever he wanted."[22]

⋇

In 1956, '57 and '62, Webster took part in some recordings with trumpet player Harry Edison. Although Webster excelled in the ballads, the records sound routine.[23] Apparently, Edison wasn't very inspiring company. Whitney Balliett wrote of him at the time: "Edison, in recent years, has, like Bud Freeman, perfected a master solo, which he varies only slightly, regardless of tempo, material or mood. Playing with him must be like chatting with a robot."[24]

It was a few months before Webster recorded his next masterpieces. In the meantime, he played on some unremarkable recordings for RCA and Contemporary, led by Benny Carter, Barney Kessel, and Red Norvo. A more interesting record was one for Fantasy, officially starring Bill Harris but mostly dominated by Webster, which features harmonious interplay between the two wind players and pianist Jimmy Rowles. In his tone formation and plain, melodic play, Harris' approach resembled Webster's. He too had a way of subtly kneading his sound—you can actually hear him breathing and pressing the mouthpiece to his lips.[25]

On October 15 and 16, 1957, Webster made two more historic Verve recordings. He was accompanied by Oscar Peterson's orchestra, and Coleman Hawkins joined him on the second day. The recordings made the first day were released under the title *Soulville*. Webster played more relaxed here than he did on *King of the Tenors*, and the good recording quality captures every little sigh on tape.[26] His phrasing is as natural and effortless as the breathing of a sleeping child.

Webster never pushes himself; after a pause, the next phrase does not follow until he is completely ready for it. Musicians who try to write down and reproduce his solos in "Makin' Whoopee," "Soulville," and "Lover Come Back to Me" will realize how logically his improvisations are constructed. Any change, the omission of any note, or a pause anywhere at all would detract from the piece as a whole—the sign of a fully realized work of art.

At both sessions, light-fingered Oscar Peterson accommodates the tenor players with bluesy riffs that perfectly complement their solos. Webster voiced his appreciation. "There are pianists who get in your way, but Oscar never does that, so I don't need to worry

about a thing. One of the things I admire about him: he can get real busy when he's doing a solo, but when it's your turn, he plays just for you."[27]

Ray Brown's majestic bass notes offer not only the perfect harmonic and rhythmic basis, but are melodies in themselves. Paul Chambers had the best timing of all bass players, and Oscar Pettiford was the most talented soloist, but Brown outdid them both when it came to constructing bass lines.

In the Hawkins duets, it is clear that Ben has become his former idol's equal. On "It Never Entered My Mind" he even outdoes Hawkins. A typical harmonic improviser, Hawkins doesn't get many chances to go all out because of the limited number of chord transitions. He sounds a little put out after his colleague's magnificently executed melody.

Hawkins has a generally sharper sound, trusts his instincts less, and tries to assert himself more. His technique is better, and he tends to be more adventurous. But when it comes to expressing melancholy, he cannot equal Ben. Webster considered these two records his best work under Granz (always excepting that Tatum record).

One of the highlights is "You'd Be So Nice To Come Home To," where the two tenorists share the stage and drummer Alvin Stoller beats exactly the right medium tempo. The Latin number "La Rosita" gets beautifully kitschy when Hawkins and Webster launch into a two-voiced melody.

Webster recalled that this last piece was a little problematic. "That number is in E, which is a really difficult key for sax players. Hawk said, 'Ben, I'll take the first slow part, and where it starts swinging, you'll take over.' I said, 'There's no way I'm going to swing in E major tonight!' Because that would give him all the time he needed to play his chords, and I'd have to do all the hard work. But then we started laughing, and we decided to go ahead and do it after all."[28]

The most moving piece of jazz television of all time was made in December 1957. On the program *The Sound of Jazz*, Billie Holiday sang her blues "Fine and Mellow," accompanied by not just Lester Young, but Hawkins and

opposite: Webster on The Sound of Jazz program, 1957.

Webster as well. Young and Holiday, both of whom were to die within two years, produced the most touching moments, musically as well as visually. Webster added succinct solos to the broadcast and to the rehearsal (both were released on record).[29]

None of the three 1958 sessions with Johnny Hodges are must-haves for Webster fans. The repertoire consists mostly of blues, with predictably evolving solos, and themes the composer can't have labored over very long.[30]

The Soul of Ben Webster and *Ben Webster and Associates* are not much better. Most of the music has the character of a routine jam session—an impression that besets many recordings from this decade. The themes, on-the-spot improvisations over the blues chords, demonstrate that Webster wasn't a born composer either.[31]

※

In November 1958, *Down Beat* journalist Leonard Feather subjected Ben Webster to a blindfold test. "As one of those musicians inclined to be kindly disposed to fellow jazzmen, Webster was a little reluctant to take a Blindfold Test. Once involved, however, he evinced a great interest in the proceedings. A couple of the items played were stereo records, and he was full of inquiries about the nature and quality of the hi-fi rig. During several of the numbers, he was jumping up and down, checking on the keys of the performances (and revealing that he has absolute pitch)."

It is notable that Webster didn't make a single mistake in identifying the musicians. When Feather played an album by Bud Shank and Bob Cooper, two West Coast reed players, he said, "What style do they call this—cool? People sneak in with 'West Coast' and 'Chicago' style, but music is music—swingin'." About Sonny Rollins, one of the most progressive musicians of the day: "I always did dig Sonny because when he was coming on in the mid-forties, most of the kids had a small sound, and Sonny always tried to have a bigger sound... The tenor is a big horn, and you should get a big sound out of it."

The highest rating (fifty stars, even though the prescribed maximum was five) went to the records by Ella Fitzgerald with Ellington, and Chu Berry with Roy Eldridge. "Roy and Chu could accomplish one thing that I could never accomplish. The piano player could play the wrong changes or the bass player could play the wrong changes, and they get their scene going right through—they break right through... I couldn't do that. If I don't get the right bass, I'm dead."[32]

⁂

In November and December 1959, two more Verve records followed: one with Peterson's group, and one with Gerry Mulligan. The first is a real gem and may even surpass *Soulville*, the earlier Peterson record on which Webster is the only wind player.[33] The record with Mulligan does not reach quite the same level, but does contain commendable solos and relaxed interplay with the resourceful baritone sax player.[34]

These were his last important sessions for Norman Granz. Ben's financial situation went downhill fast from there. He was not a very good businessman, had that alcohol problem, and was reluctant to adapt his music to current trends. So he was hit hard when Granz stopped organizing U.S. concerts in 1957, and sold the Verve label in 1960. Granz moved to Switzerland and organized concerts from there, but virtually all were outside the States.

In 1967 he did organize one American tour, with such artists as Coleman Hawkins and Benny Carter. It also included his two favorites, "Ella & Oscar," who had kept him on as their personal manager. After this concert session, he announced, "Never again. I made a profit, but it's too much of a production, too much work, and above all, too much aggravation... There's more stability in Europe. You find the same successful people still enjoying the same reaction... I've been bringing Ray Charles over every year for five years, Ella and Oscar annually for much longer."[35]

Webster was not one of the lucky few who could count on Granz' continued support after his emigration. The organizer usually brought only the very biggest stars to Europe, and he didn't consider Webster to belong to that class.

Granz: "Ben was limited as a sax player... He never got to Hawkins' musical level. Not at all. Every time I did a session with him, he'd come in and say, 'I asked Coleman over as well.' And I'd ask him, 'Why did you do that—that guy will tear you into ribbons.' And one time he asked Budd Johnson as well! That guy could kill anyone. [Granz is talking about *Ben Webster and Associates* here, the session that took place on April 9, 1959.]

"Roy Eldridge was there too, and Roy said to me, 'Ben is crazy, why did he bring Budd Johnson and Hawk along? God knows what he thinks he's doing.' To make things worse, he let them play the first solos as well. By the time Hawkins and Budd Johnson were finished, there was nothing left to play for Webster. It was insane. But as long as Webster played in a medium tempo, he could swing. His timing was fantastic. And his ballads were beautiful of course. During that session with Art Tatum, Art just could not get Ben to speed up. Ben just did his own thing. So up to a point, Art adapted to Ben there. Now if Art had had someone like Coleman Hawkins in front of him, someone who was his equal harmonically... Or someone like Dizzy, with his speed, now that would have been great for Art too."[36]

※

In the fall of 1957 Webster moved back to the East Coast. He found an affordable room in Miss Sutton's boarding house on Long Island—the same place where tenor saxophonist Harold Ashby lodged. Ashby and Ben had been good friends ever since meeting in Kansas City in 1949.

Ashby: "I've admired his music from the moment I first heard him play with Duke Ellington. I was fifteen at the time, and my older brother had taken me to a theater in Kansas City. At Ben's recommendation, I also moved into Miss Sutton's house on Long Island. It was quite a train ride from Manhattan, but it was quiet and peaceful, nicer than all that big-town noise.

"Ben has helped me a lot. He let me play on his record,

The Soul of Ben Webster. And it was through him that I met Duke Ellington. Ben took me over to the Apollo theater and introduced me to The Duke. And that's why I got to substitute a few times in Ellington's band back then. About ten years later, in 1968, Ellington hired me as a permanent player. That made me Ben's indirect successor in the band. I consider that a great honor, because Ben was my first and biggest inspiration."

While the 32-year-old Ashby was gradually building his career, Webster found he was past his prime. He got paid less than he used to for studio work, and club gigs were hard to come by. Webster had gotten accustomed to the high rates Granz paid, so he turned down some gigs that paid less well. At the time, he didn't realize that he was digging his own grave.

He'd often end up playing with artists that couldn't even stand in his shadow artistically—just like back in the 52nd Street days. On the October 1958 album *At the Nuway Club* he can be heard in such company. The album was recorded at a regular Sunday afternoon session in a Long Island club, with amateur quality recording equipment.[37]

The musicians remembered that, whenever he did get a gig, Webster would bring along his own tape recorder. He often went to Queens to visit guitar player Jimmy Cannady, the leader of the Nuway Club house orchestra. "Ben practically lived at my place in those days. He'd come over for dinner and bring his tape recorder, and then he'd settle in and listen to music, looking for interesting discoveries."[38]

In April, 1958, he suddenly got some work at the Village Vanguard. In this New York club he spent two weeks playing with Jimmy Jones on piano, Joe Benjamin on bass, and Dave Bailey on drums. According to Whitney Balliett, this was his first New York performance in over a decade. He called it a "lugubrious spectacle." "He was playing magnificently, but the audiences, made up largely of musicians and mourners, were scarce, and Webster's run was not extended. A short time later, he surfaced again at a Czechoslovakian bar, on Second Avenue in the Seventies, and on one poignant night he played to a house of five people—this reviewer and two friends, and what appeared to be a couple of Webster's relatives."[39]

Not long after, he found a few nights' employment at the Metropole, this time with drummer Denzil Best (who stopped playing soon after because of health problems), and some lesser deities: Earl Knight on piano and Carl Pruitt on bass. In the fall of 1959, he gave up on the New York scene and returned home to Mayme and Mom at Wilton Place in L.A.

On his last night in New York, he went for a walk with jazz reporter Dan Morgenstern. "He spoke, without a trace of resentment, about his disappointment with the big city. One of his main points was the difficulty in keeping a group together when steady work was not forthcoming, and the heartbreak of having to disband a unit just when a few weeks together had made everything 'nice and tight.' "[40]

It wouldn't be until 1973 that Granz got back into the

record business, when he founded the record label Pablo. Webster never benefited from Granz' comeback; he died that same year.

notes

1 From the movie *The Brute and the Beautiful*, by John Jeremy (1989).

2 "Chelsea Bridge" can be heard on, for instance, *The Soul Of Ben Webster*, Verve.

3 *The New Yorker*, January 19, 1963.

4 *Walter Brown with Jay McShann's Band*, Affinity, and *The Complete Ben Webster on EmArcy*, EmArcy.

5 Examples of this studio gigs from this period can be found on *The Complete Ben Webster on EmArcy*, EmArcy.

6 See note 5.

7 See note 5.

8 *Down Beat*, July 15, 1942.

9 Nat Shapiro and Nat Hentoff (edd.), *The Jazz Makers* (Rhinehart 1957); republished by Da Capo, 1979.

10 Various Artists: *JATP in Tokyo*, Pablo.

11 *Charlie Parker Jam Session*, Verve.

12 See note 5.

13 *Live*, Jazz Anthology.

14 *King of the Tenors*, Verve.

15 Gunther Schuller, *The Swing Era* (Oxford University Press 1989).

16 *Music With Feeling*, Verve.

17 Billie Holiday, *All or Nothing At All*, Verve. Part of the first session with Holiday can be found on *Billie Holiday/ Compact Jazz*, Verve.

18 Billie Holiday: *Body and Soul*, Verve, and *Songs for Distingué Lovers*, Verve.

19 *Art Tatum/Ben Webster Quartet*, Pablo.

20 See note 1.

21 *Jazz Hot*, September 1972.

22 *Jazz Magazine*, May 1965.

23 Harry Edison: *Sweets*, Verve; *Blues for Basie*, Verve; and *Ben Webster & Sweets Edison*, Columbia.
24 *The New Yorker*, January 19, 1963.
25 *Bill Harris and Friends*, Fantasy/Milestone.
26 *Soulville*, Verve; and *Coleman Hawkins Encounters Ben Webster*, Verve 823120-2 (CD).
27 Cover text on the album *Blues for Basie* (see note 23).
28 Bert Vuijsje, *Jazzportretten* (Van Gennep 1983).
29 Billie Holiday: *Broadcast Performances*, ESP (the broadcast); various Artists: *The Sound of Jazz*, CBS 57036 (CD) (the rehearsal).
30 Johnny Hodges: *Blues a Plenty*, Verve; Duke Ellington/ Johnny Hodges: *Side By Side*, Verve; and Johnny Hodges: *Not So Dukish*, Verve.
31 *The Soul of Ben Webster*: see note 2; *Ben Webster and Associates*, Verve.
32 *Down Beat*, November 27, 1958.
33 *Ben Webster Meets Oscar Peterson*, Verve.
34 *Gerry Mulligan Meets Ben Webster*, Verve.
35 Leonard Feather, *From Satchmo to Miles* (Stein and Day 1972); later reissued by Quartet Books.
36 *De Volkskrant*, July 13, 1984.
37 *At The Nuway Club*, Jazz Guild.
38 Cover text to the album *At The Nuway Club*, see note 37.
39 *The New Yorker*, Janury 19, 1963.
40 *Jazz Journal*, January, 1964.

final years in the states

Guitar player Jim Hall: "After I finally left the Jimmy Giuffre Trio, in 1959, I went back to the West Coast, and I was in a band Ben had with Jimmy Rowles [piano] and Red Mitchell [bass] and Frank Butler [drums]. We worked for a while in a club on the Strip called the Renaissance, and at first I didn't get paid. Then I think everybody in the band chipped something in. Anyway, Ben and I hung out a lot. He didn't have a car, and he lived with his mother and grandmother [Hall meant his great-aunt, of course] way over on the other side of L.A., but he'd never ask me to pick him up. What he'd do is call me whenever we had a gig and say, 'We'll meet at my house first...'

"One evening when I went to get him, he was stretched out on the sofa snoring—the whole works. He must have been up all night, and we couldn't budge him. He had a reputation of taking a sock at whoever tried to wake him.

"So his mother and grandmother would lean over him and say, 'Ben, Mr. Hall is here and it's time to go to work,' and then jump back about two feet. I finally suggested that I get a wet towel or something, and they looked at me with their mouths open, and said, 'Oh no, he don't like *any* surprises.'

"Ben was very melodramatic, and he talked in that big voice just the way he played. Another time I went to get him he had a washcloth on top of his head and he was shaving. Some Art Tatum records were on and he kept running out of the bathroom and mimicking fantastic Tatum figures. Then he started telling me what Tatum was like—he loved to talk about the great ones he knew who were gone—and the next thing I knew he was crying.

"I never saw any of the meanness he was famous for, except once he fell asleep in the front seat of my car and when I woke him he cursed me. But the next minute he apologized."[1]

※

Not long after Ben moved to L.A., he decided to content himself with the status of sideman. He went to work for Jimmy Witherspoon ("Spoon" to friends), a blues singer with jazzy inflections. Some weeks after they started working together, disc jockey and festival organizer Jimmy Lions asked Witherspoon to perform at the 1959 Monterey Jazz Festival.

The immediate cause for this was a record Witherspoon made earlier that year (without Webster) for the California label World Pacific. This was a wonderful offer, because the singer had been performing in small, seedy clubs for years. His livelihood was also under constant

opposite: Jimmy Witherspoon

threat from rock 'n' roll stars like Elvis Presley. Witherspoon realized that this was his chance for a breakthrough. He would share the stage with a one-time formation that also starred Hawkins, Eldridge, and pianist Earl Hines. It turned into a showy evening: at the end of the night he stepped up on stage, hit the piano twice with his palm and barked, " 'Down Home!' A flat!" He then grabbed the microphone and sang the blues for about six thousand people. He had them at his feet in no time. Webster excelled in "Ain't Nobody's Business." The public cheered. "Ben wrote his name tonight," the singer solemnly pronounced after the show was over.

After this triumph, Witherspoon and his men soon found better-paying gigs, and Webster realized he had bet on the right horse. Said Witherspoon, "For me, Ben Webster was number one. After the Monterey Festival, we stayed together for almost three years. We never took a job if the other didn't get hired too."[2]

On the cover of their last record together, the singer says, "Ben and I both have a reputation of being arrogant and troublemakers. So everybody expected trouble when we formed a group together. But we have never had even a single fight, never said an unpleasant word to each other."

The Monterey concert was brought out on record, and was followed by five more albums featuring the duo. Each has its own distinct character. A session at the Renaissance club on December 2, 1959, is remarkable for Mulligan's intelligent solos. A week later, Webster and Witherspoon performed with the rocking trio of pianist Vince Guaraldi. The best sessions are probably the last ones, on May 23, 1962. The tempos are generally slower, giving both Spoon and Webster the opportunity to put a lot of expression into their work.[3]

This last record concludes with "Please, Mister Webster"—a variation on "Please, Mister Johnson," a well-known piece among blues artists. The sax player reaches the level of his finest Peterson recordings. Spoon sings "Please, Mister Webster, don't play those blues so sad," a request which is fortunately ignored. When listening to this record especially, you'll hear that the sax player doesn't rely on the typical blues licks in the slower tempos; he often solos as though the number were a ballad.

The collaboration was drawing to its natural end. It was nice for Webster to play with a successful group that didn't go on long tours, and didn't ask much more of him than to show up on time and play the odd blues solo. However, the repertoire consisted almost entirely of twelve-bar blues, and Spoon's range of musical emotions was limited. As a result, Webster's inspiration would sometimes flag.

Other than his work with Witherspoon, the West Coast didn't have much to offer Ben. Leonard Feather: "California didn't show any gratitude for Ben's presence. He had little more to do than the occasional record gig or club session. Everybody was talking about his beautiful warm sound; everybody admired him and patted him on the back, but Hollywood is sometimes long on backpats and short on gigs."[4]

According to producer Lester Koenig, Webster hung around Los Angeles anyway because Mayme and Mom, who were in their 90s and 80s then, weren't doing well. "Their health got worse, and he was worried about them all the time."[5]

There were some small gigs—one, for instance, with Jim Hall in The Renaissance, as well as studio sessions where he provided background for singers like Jo Stafford, Big Miller, Jimmy Rushing, Kay Starr, Helen Humes, and Anita O'Day. The latter also happened to be the person he made his last Verve recording with.

In about half the pieces on the Humes record, Webster plays solos which, though short, are not without merit. The same applies to most of the other sessions. The average jazz lover would probably not buy them specifically for Webster's contributions, however.[6] A more interesting record is *That Healin' Feeling* starring organist "Groove" Holmes—a record that really swings.[7]

In 1961 and '62, some recordings for Frank Sinatra's Reprise label followed. The results were disappointing. One of them, a record "with strings," appeared under the name *The Warm Moods*, and contains something close to elevator music.[8] During one session with Sinatra, Webster got barely any solo space at all. His only satisfactory record for Reprise is the final album with Witherspoon (originally issued on Reprise).

At Ben's request, Lester Koening, of the Contemporary label, recorded an evening at the Renaissance. This was October 14, 1960, just over a week after the recording with Humes. Unfortunately, the sound quality leaves a lot to be desired because the technician was seated right behind the stage, separated from the musicians by no more than a curtain. This is a shame, because the music that night was excellent. The CD version contains an extra half-hour of music of even worse recording quality than the rest.[9]

※

The piano player at the Renaissance, Jimmy Rowles, had been a close friend of Ben's ever since the Ellington years. Rowles had moved to L.A. as well by now, and the two often worked together. Rowles recalled, "I first met him in Tacoma, near Seattle, where he was playing with Ellington. During the intermission, I walked over to him and introduced myself. He said, 'Where is the shithouse?' That was the first thing he said to me. After that night, the band stayed in Seattle for a two-week gig. Every night, after his work was done, I would go jamming with him. I felt very privileged, because there wasn't much of a jazz scene out there.

"Ben said, 'I'll make sure you get to play for Benny Goodman.' And he kept his word, because thanks to his recommendation, I ended up playing for Goodman about two years later. Later on, in Los Angeles, we'd play a lot of golf together. He always called me Shithouse, in memory of our first meeting. After a while, I started calling him Shithouse as well. In company, we'd keep it decent and call each other S.H."

Shortly after the final recording with Witherspoon on May 23, 1960, Webster traveled back to the East Coast to try his luck there one more time. The immediate reason was a guest spot at the Washington Jazz Festival with Roy Eldridge and Oscar Peterson's trio. At musicologist Gunther Schuller's urging, he was brought out to Washington at the last minute, and witnesses recalled that he gladly seized the opportunity.

After the festival, he visited New York, where he made a record with Harry Edison mentioned in chapter 6. He also played in the Shalimar club for a week, a fun place with cheap drinks. An unfortunate result of these low prices was that musicians had to make do with a small paycheck and a tin-kettle piano. The interest in his work wasn't exactly overwhelming—so it was back to L.A.

In California, he learned that Mayme and Mom's health had deteriorated even further. They could no longer take care of themselves, let alone pamper their boy Benjamin Francis. They both had to move to a nursing home, and Ben was left in the Wilton Place house by himself. He fell into a depression and turned to the bottle even more. There were hardly any club gigs, and no studio work whatsoever in this last period in L.A.

According to his second cousin Joyce Cockrell, "Ben wasn't getting the jobs he used to do. He was getting fat and was drinking very heavily and got brutal sometimes. He could hardly get along with anybody. He was scared to death that Mayme and mom would die... And he realised he was losing his popularity."[10]

In the first six months of 1963, Ben's mother Mayme and his great-aunt Agnes Johnson both died in the nursing home. They were both in their 90s—Johnson, in fact, would have turned one hundred the following year. Ben asked Joyce and his cousin Harley to sell the house, and once more moved back to New York.

He arrived in the Big Apple in June of 1963. He was full of good resolutions, and judging from the lack of alcohol stories from this period, he must have managed to control himself for a time. He kicked off this New York stay with another stint at the Shalimar. This time, business was better. Journalists in the audience—including Stanley Dance and Dan Morgenstern—had good things to say about him, and by all accounts he performed brilliantly.

One night he was accompanied by Patti Bown on piano, Richard Davis on bass, and Grady Tate on drums. The latter was a temporary replacement for Mel Lewis, who finished the rest of the Shalimar gig. Lewis had also moved from Los Angeles to New York in this period, tired of the boring studio work and looking for musical challenges. The moment he got to New York, the drummer started singing Webster's praises everywhere—something Ben needed at that time especially.

Morgenstern: "Relaxed and in full command of himself and the situation, he charged into "Cotton Tail" with all the old fire—and then some. He brought stars into the eyes of the pretty girls at the bar with "My Romance," and silenced all idle chatter with his inimitable rendition of "Danny Boy"."[11]

The quartet was only supposed to play in the Shalimar for a week, but was so popular that they ended up staying for six. Bown had other obligations, and was replaced by David Frishberg at some point. After this success, several other interesting offers came streaming in, so the newly formed trio—Frishberg, Davis and Lewis—wound up playing with him for the next six months. The Ben Webster Quartet did a concert at Philharmonic Hall, and spent three weeks headlining at the Half Note. This was followed by gigs in the Village Vanguard, another month at the Half Note, and two weeks in Birdland at the end of the year.

The jazz scene loved him. He got rave reviews, and a chance to meet up with old friends. When the Ellington band was in town for a short while, Billy Strayhorn, Johnny Hodges, and Paul Gonsalves joined the quartet at the Half Note. Webster also got a chance to hear Hawkins, who was playing the Village Gate.

David Frishberg describes this period: "By the time I knew Ben, he was in his mid-50s, and the fabled brawler had disappeared. He was just an excessively sentimental guy. He cried every time he mentioned his mother. But he really took charge on the bandstand. He never told us outright what he wanted to play. He'd hum a bar and start, or he'd just go '*Blam! Blam!*' and we were supposed to know what he was going to do. I made some mistakes at first, but after a week or so I learned to translate the hums and blams."[12]

In August 1963, Ben left his hotel and spent several months at pianist Joe Zawinul's house at 382 Central Park West. Hawkins' apartment was at number 372, so the old tenor player was their neighbor. Zawinul, later world-famous as one of the founders of the fusion group

Weather Report, had recently joined Cannonball Adderley's popular band.

The originally-Viennese pianist and the Kansas City tenor player had met earlier that year in California. Zawinul was working there with Adderley, and he met Webster in the club next door, where he had a gig with Witherspoon.

Zawinul: "Shortly after I had moved to New York, I had to go to Japan on a tour with Cannonball. I saw Ben in Birdland, and asked him if he'd like to stay at my house during that time. When I returned, he was still there. He had paid half the rent, and wanted to stay. I thought that was fine, because the house was too big for just me anyway. Hawkins regularly came by, and we'd have jam sessions, just the three of us."

He told Peter Keepnews [reported in an album's liner notes]: "I had an arrangement of "Come Sunday" which we did with Cannonball. It was pretty complicated. Ben had me write it down for him. He said, 'When Coleman comes in, we'll play this for him, and give him a nice surprise!' Another day, Hawkins took me aside in the elevator and said, 'Why don't you come over to my house so we can practice some nice fast pieces'—because he knew that Ben wasn't that good with fast pieces. They were always trying to one-up each other."[13]

Unlike Ben, Hawkins kept trying to remain the young, hip guy. Shortly after Hawkins' death, on May 19, 1969, Webster said that, "I'm not a hundred percent sure that Hawkins was only sixty-four when he died. About eight years ago, Roy [Eldridge], Hawk and I went drinking in a bar in New York... Hawk said to Roy, 'When I was a little boy, my dad would take me out to go listen to Ben Webster.' I said, 'Come off it, Bean!' But he didn't smile. He pulled his cabaret card out of his pocket and showed it to us. It said, 'Age: 42.' Roy literally fell to the floor laughing, but Bean stayed perfectly composed."[14]

In general, Webster was perfectly polite to Hawkins, whom he still considered his superior. "Coleman Hawkins was a master musician—he was incredibly creative. That man has played things he has forgotten about himself, but which are still being copied today... I believe Roy Eldridge was his best friend. I was actually a little jealous of him, because I wish I'd been such a good friend of Bean's."[15]

Besides Hawkins, Roy Eldridge and Dizzy Gillespie were also regulars at Zawinul's house, so the 31-year-old pianist got to know the older musicians and their habits very well. "Never buy anything cheap," Webster once said to him, in all seriousness. "How can you be a great musician if you don't buy expensive things?"[16]

During the second engagement at the Half Note, Ben finally got to record an album as a leader. The last records under his own name—not counting the strings album for Reprise—had been the records with Mulligan and Peterson, four years earlier. The new offer came from Orrin Keepnews of Riverside, and Webster asked Richard Davis, Zawinul, and Philly Joe Jones to accompany him. The latter was not his regular drummer, but he would often substitute. At a second session for the same record, Cannonball sideman Sam Jones was added on bass, as well as cornet player Thad Jones.

The leader is in pretty good form here. Zawinul reveals himself as a skilled pianist who hasn't quite found his own style yet. Other than that, the accompaniment is flawless, and "Come Sunday" is naturally part of the selection.[17]

In the fall, Webster had to move again. Zawinul: "He was a really nice guy, but after a while the house became too small anyway. I met a nice girl who I married, and am still married to. So I said, 'Ben, you're going to have to find another place to live.' He reacted very disappointed, didn't understand why he had to leave. He was obviously not used to being shown the door."

※

Toward the end of 1963, the public's interest in Ben began to wane. Had they already heard enough of him in New York? Persistent rumors have it that he spoilt a lot of gigs through his drunkenness. Reliable critics' reports from this period, however, don't mention this even once. Whitney Balliett wrote: "Webster...is not especially erratic; he simply fluctuates between the excellent and the superb."[18]

But Balliett found that the Half Note was rarely more than one-third full during Ben's final engagement. Webster jammed his heart out, but now had a difficult time finding employment in clubs. It was the same story everywhere: all the good places had already employed him for a while, and told him to call back in a couple of years.

Before he left the country, there was only one more studio session that he led, and a few that featured him as guest soloist. He was in his 50s now, an old man by the standards of his time, and musicians of his generation were simply no longer fashionable. Many embarked on second careers as studio musicians, but that wasn't for Ben.

Milt Hinton, who played on more than a thousand albums as a sideman, explained: "Some very talented guys never made it in the studios... Ben Webster couldn't bring himself to get to a morning date on time. And in the record business nobody ever bawled you out for being late—they just didn't call you again."[19]

Ben was still full of hope when Stanley Dance came to his hotel to interview him one morning in the first half of 1964. At the beginning of the interview, he was playing his usual "wakin' up music"—Art Tatum, and stride pianists like James P. Johnson, Willie "The Lion" Smith, and Fats Waller. This was a habit he picked up in the fifties, and would continue until the end of his life.

The Ellington sidemen Ernie Sheppard and Sam Woodyard, who Webster was lucky enough to count as his neighbors, came by that day and listened to the music. Dance: " 'There's nothing happening on the West Coast anyway,' he claims, and now he regards himself as more or less permanently based in the East. He hasn't yet moved his entire collection of tapes and records, but those he has with him are well varied and include, for instance, Stravinsky's *Firebird Suite* and Kodâly's *Sonata for Unaccompanied Cello, Opus 8.*"[20]

⁂

In the course of 1964, he got into serious financial trouble. He now had the status of a B-list musician, but refused to adapt his rates. His spending pattern didn't alter either. After all, didn't he tell Zawinul never to buy anything cheap? After the summer, he was forced to move in with Milt Hinton.

Hinton: "He was hardly working anymore because he asked too much money. He even had to leave his hotel. So I said: 'You can stay at my basement, we will have some fun.' It was delightful having Ben stay with us. When I had a couple of hours off, I would get my bass and he would sit on the couch on which he slept too. We'll have a little jam session and turn on the tape recorder. We would start with an old number, and when we made a mistake or couldn't finish, we would be laughing.

"One day, somebody called for a record date. And I cautiously said: 'Well, Ben Webster is here.' And he said: 'Oh really? You think he would like to make the date?' And Ben came to the phone and said: 'I want triple scale.' And the man said: 'I'm sorry, we can't pay that.' And he hung up. I made that date and I made two more dates that day. So I made triple by making three record dates.

"And my wife said to Ben, very kindly, because she liked him, 'Ben, how can you sit here all day? Milt is just a bass player and you're a star. You sit here and eat and drink, and people offer you a job and you won't take it. Milt worked nine hours for the same money you didn't make.' I think that really broke his heart. And the first offer he got to go to Europe, he accepted it."[21]

The gig was in London. Webster had never been to Europe, but Ronnie Scott, the owner of London's largest jazz club, thought it was time to change that. Scott, also a tenor saxophonist by trade: "It was an old wish of mine to have him play here and to get to know him. Ever since those Ellington records he's been one of my idols. I loved pieces like "Cotton Tail" and "Chelsea Bridge." And his ballads were heavenly... He was one of the classic tenorists: Coleman Hawkins, Lester Young, Ben Webster."[22]

The engagement was to begin in mid-December 1964, and would last about a month. Ben traveled by boat because he was afraid of flying—the JATP tour to Japan had been torture to him. Webster would never return to the United States.

※

In spite of the lack of offers, his final New York period did yield a reasonable number of albums, mainly because some Rhode Island concerts were later released on record. *Live at Pio's*, which probably dates back to 1963, contains a half-hour of Junior Mance playing bluesy, Petersonesque piano, with pleasant—if predictable—Webster solos.[23]

In the summer of 1964, he returned to Rhode Island. He spent a few nights playing with, among others, pianist Michael Renzi. The results were released on three albums. One of these appeared partially under the name of singer Carol Sloane, who guested one day at Webster's request.

Too much of a good thing, it soon turned out. The recording quality varies from mediocre to bad—disastrous for a soloist like Webster, whose tone is easily as important as his notes. The accompaniment is nothing special, and Ben doesn't get much further than rattling off his own clichés. Young Carol Sloane appears to be—as far as the poor sound quality allows one to judge—a competent singer who has listened closely to Ella Fitzgerald.[24]

In March of 1964 he recorded *See You at the Fair*, his best record since the session with Peterson he led in November 1959. "Stardust," "Someone to Watch Over Me," and "Over the Rainbow" are rendered in a sober, impressive way. The sidemen's solos are no longer than strictly necessary, and are sometimes omitted altogether—a relief after these interminable live recordings.[25]

It was probably Milt Hinton who managed to get him into a few recording sessions in 1963 and 1964, with Clark Terry, Lionel Hampton, and singers Joe Williams and Sylvia Syms. He only plays the entire sessions in the case of Hampton and Terry. *The Happy Horns of Clark Terry* consists of nice arrangements that don't give the tenor sax much room for improvisation.[26] Hampton's *You Better Know It!!!* is more interesting. Supported by the superior rhythm duo Milt Hinton and Osie Johnson, the sextet plays a number of the vibraphonist's old and new favorites. There are a lot of tenor solos and the record has been well planned out, so it distinguishes itself from the many predictable, somewhat lazy recordings Webster had recently done.[27]

On November 10 or 11, 1964, Ben spent his last day in an American studio. He played parts in two pieces on Oliver Nelson's *More Blues and the Abstract Truth*. Nelson was trying to give the old blues a facelift here while still honoring the true blues spirit—and the attempt largely succeeds.

Webster plays it safe on "Midnight Blue," but manages to hold one's attention on the melancholy "Blues for Mister Broadway" (which is only partly a blues). The accompanying musicians are not playing their usual clichés here, which seems to inspire him.[28]

Probably at a slightly later date—Hinton mentioned "right before Ben left for Europe"—some five minutes of clumsy piano play were recorded in Milt Hinton's basement, as well as two informal duets with Hinton: "All The Things You Are" and "Sophisticated Lady." Hinton recorded this music with his tape recorder, and gave the tapes to producer Harry Lim after Webster died.[29]

notes

1 Whitney Balliet, *American Musicians* (Oxford University Press 1986).

2 *Jazz Times*, January 1964.

3 The sessions at the Monterey Festival and those with Mulligan can be found on Jimmy Witherspoon/Gerry Mulligan: *The 'Spoon Concerts*, Fantasy; the session with Guaraldi on *Jimmy Witherspoon & Ben Webster*, Verve; and the final one on *Jimmy Witherspoon & Ben Webster*, WB Records.

4 Cover text to Benny Carter: *Opening Blues*, Prestige.

5 Cover text to the album *At the Renaissance*, Contemporary.
6 Helen Humes: *Songs I Like To Sing*, Contemporary.
7 Reissued as *Richard Groove Holmes with Ben Webster: Groove*, Pacific Jazz.
8 *The Warm Moods*, reissued as Discovery.
9 *At The Renaissance*, Contemporary.
10 From the movie *The Brute and the Beautiful*, by John Jeremy (1989).
11 *Jazz Journal*, January 1964.
12 See note 1.
13 Cover text to the two album set *Trav'lin Light*, Milestone M-47056.
14 Bert Vuijsje, *Jazzportretten* (Van Gennep 1983). Hawkins was actually born November 21, 1904.
15 See note 14.
16 See note 13.
17 *Soulmates*, Original Jazz Classics.
18 *The New Yorker*, August 17, 1963.
19 Milt Hinton and David G. Berger, *Bass Line* (Temple University Press 1988).
20 Stanley Dance, *The World of Duke Ellington* (Charles Schribner's Sons 1970/1981).
21 See note 10.
22 See note 10.
23 *Tenor Giants/Live at Pio's*, Enja.
24 *Live! Providence, Rhode Island*, Storyville; and *Carol & Ben*, HoneyDew HD 6608 (all LPs).
25 *See You at the Fair*, Impulse.
26 Clark Terry: *The Happy Horns of Clark Terry*, Impulse.
27 Lionel Hampton: *You better Know It!!!*, Impulse.
28 Oliver Nelson: *More Blues and the Abstract Truth*, Impulse.
29 Milt Hinton: *Here Swings the Judge*, Famous Door HL-104 (LP).

a new life in europe

Mid-December, 1964, Ben arrived in London for a month-long gig at the jazz club that bore the name of its owner, Ronnie Scott. His rhythm section consisted of Stan Tracey on piano, Rick Laird on bass, and Jackie Dougan on drums. He soon got used to playing with these musicians, judging by the television program *Jazz 625*, which aired on December 20.[1]

Ronnie Scott: "He was nice to be with, he made friends. He was staying at the White House, Albany Street, in a small flat were he always had some guests about. He was of course received with great admiration. The jazz musicians here and the local jazz fans were crazy about to him because he was such a big name.

"I believe he had a good time in London. He often went to Dobell, the big jazz record store. The employees loved him. He'd go there on a regular basis, and just sit around talking to the customers. His fans went there to meet him. Especially Henny Cohen, our doorman. I always said, 'Henny must be eating furniture for dinner.' Ben wasn't a small guy either, and the two were really close. We always thought he'd return to the States after that month, but things turned out differently."[2]

More offers began coming in. Webster seemed to be realizing what had probably been his goal all along: building a new life for himself in Europe. He played in a few more places in the U.K., gave concerts in Sweden, at the Metropole in Oslo, and then continued on to Copenhagen.

He liked it here. The city was beautiful, and he found regular employment at the Montmartre club with one of Europe's best rhythm sections: pianist Kenny Drew, 18-year-old bass player Niels-Henning Ørsted-Pedersen, and 24-year-old drummer Alex Riel. Drew had emigrated from the United States to Europe in 1961, and had been living in Copenhagen for the last few months. This was the trio Ben made his first European record with on January 30 and 31.[3]

He also met up with an old friend: Ole Brask, a photographer with whom he had spent a lot of time during his last years in New York. In Copenhagen, Brask sometimes acted as his manager. He also introduced him to many local jazz enthusiasts.

Webster: "There's people there [in Copenhagen] who really love music... When I first got there, I already knew Ole Brask. He was a good friend of Timme's [Timme Rosenkrantz, a Danish jazz fan and producer], who is sadly no longer among us—he rests in peace. Ole was a great support for me, because when you're new in town, and you don't know anybody, you need some help."[4]

From Copenhagen he made a number of small tours. In April he played in Paris with Mal Waldron; in May he got a guest engagement with English trumpet player Humphrey Lyttelton's band—a second guest here was trumpet player Buck Clayton—and at the end of June, he was invited to work at Ronnie Scott's for the second time. In between these travels he stayed in Copenhagen, where he could often be found at the Montmartre—not only to play, but simply to have a beer and talk with friends and admirers.

※

Like many American jazz musicians, in Europe Ben found the acknowledgement he missed. But in one respect he reverted to the conditions of twenty years before, when he fronted his own combos on 52nd Street—he had to play with mediocre, sometimes downright pitiful musicians.

In these years, American musicians used the expression "a European rhythm section" for an accompanying group that let the tempo slow down or hurried it on, and made it impossible to swing. At the moment I'm writing this—in 2000—European musicians have largely caught up with American ones, but back then they still had a lot to learn.

During the last nine years of his life, Webster's residence alternated between Copenhagen and Amsterdam. Both cities had at least one good rhythm section. Copenhagen had the trio of Drew/NHØP/Riel, Amsterdam hosted a trio of pianist Cees Slinger, bass player Jacques Schols (sometimes replaced by the equally good Rob

Langereis), and drummer John Engels. Unfortunately, these musicians were not always available, so on tour Webster often had to make do with local talent.

The worst group he ever worked with was the trio that can be heard on the album *At Ease*. These are some amateurs from the north of the Netherlands, including a drummer and bass player who couldn't even get an amateur gig these days. The release of this session caused a small scandal. But more about that later.[5]

It soon became apparent that even many professional musicians were not at his level. In July 1965, *Jazz Monthly* wrote the following about a gig at Ronnie Scott's: "The pianist, Alan Branscombe, offered a bland, pre-digested pastiche of the most hackneyed current clichés... The playing of the bassist, Lennie Bush, was so nondescript that it's difficult to recall anything about it aside from his rather muddy time and boring choice of notes.

"In fact, the main fault that hampered the supporting trio, apart from their complete lack of originality and inspiration, was their very weak time. The drummer, Jackie Dougan, rushed the tempo with admirable consistency, but in fact none of the three musicians could play in time with themselves or each other, much less make the kind of subtle and meaningful use of rhythm that Webster could." Tough criticism, especially coming from the usually chauvinistic British press.

While his American records had at least passably good background musicians in the fifties and sixties, some of Ben's European albums feature painfully poor bassists and drummers. The Danish orchestra of tenorist Steen Vig, with who he played on March 19, 1965, was a stiff Dixieland outfit.[6] In January 1967, he had to make do with Allen Haven, an uninspired organist who played nothing but protracted chords.[7] The sessions on April 4 and 7, 1967, were ruined by the rhythm section of the Alex Welsh Band, a dull little group that would have discouraged any soloist with the way they drag themselves through the music.[8] And that's just the beginning of a very long list.

※

It's not surprising that, faced with this difficulty, Ben sometimes drank more than was good for him. His alcohol problem, which he had under control in his final New York years, was rearing its head again. Besides that, he was lonely. He was always surrounded by fans who greeted him with great respect, and remembered even better than he did where and with whom he made that one particular recording, twenty or thirty years earlier. But he didn't meet many kindred spirits in Europe. He was surrounded by much-younger musicians who had not grown up in Kansas City, but in Osted, Denmark, Eton, England, or Alkmaar (the Netherlands).

Egbert de Bloeme, a law student in Amsterdam at the time, remembered: "Both in Copenhagen and Amsterdam he was continually surrounded by people, but he lacked a true companion. He had hardly any family left, and his old friends lived in another country and died one after the other. It's a lonely life of course, traveling around and living in hotels or boarding houses.

The life of a famous, respected musician isn't as much fun as people might imagine."

Ole Brask once organized a concert for him in Barcelona. During the long train journey Webster, always in for a conversation, got acquainted with some fellow travelers. The friendship had to be sealed with a few drinks, and after he got a little too noisy he was escorted from the train and taken to a police station.

When he finally sobered up and awoke, he realized it was the morning after the concert was supposed to have taken place, and that he had been unable to reach Barcelona. He returned to Copenhagen, filled with remorse, and reimbursed Brask for the train trip and the missed commission.

A concert with even worse consequences for his reputation took place in late October of 1965, during the Berliner Jazztage. This festival, organized by critic Joachim Ernst Berendt, was a prominent event that attracted the attention of the entire European jazz scene. He was supposed to be part of a tenor gathering intended as the festival's high point.

Ruud Kuyper wrote in the Dutch newspaper *NRC*: "First, Brew Moore and Don Byas appeared on stage, and about a minute after the announcement, a fat man in gray pants and a blue sport coat came lumbering onto the stage. It turned out to be tenor sax player Ben Webster, who had apparently gone a little wild celebrating the congregation of so many colleagues. The man turned out to be unable to do anything with his sax at all—instead, he disturbed the other players' work, started talking to the audience, and made the strangest gestures."[9]

Jazz Wereld reported that back in the dressing room, where Ben was whining for another cognac, Berendt handed him a saxophone and gently pushed him toward the stage. He was in a great mood, but didn't seem to realize what was expected of him. And so he greeted his colleagues all over again, after which he gave an unintelligible speech in a mixture of German, French, and English.

The accompaniment (Drew, NHØP, and drummer Alan Dawson) had to repeat the introductory measures over and over again before he finally understood and started to play. What followed was an extremely brief, embarrassing little chorus. "Mr. Webster is very cheerful tonight" the nervous radio commentator managed to add before Berendt belatedly ushered Ben offstage.[10]

His drinking spoiled a number of English tours as well. Organizer Jim Godbolt: "One night he surpassed himself by striding, naked and unashamed, through a hotel corridor brandishing his knife, and tried to obtain entry into a ladies' toilet where his girlfriend was hiding. He had a penchant for ladies' toilets."[11] (As Webster didn't have a steady girlfriend at the time, this must have been some female acquaintance.)

At his London apartment—in the illustriously named White House complex, apartment 802—he threw parties that could last day and night. The other tenants were not amused. British journalist Max Jones tried to keep an eye on Ben by taking him over to his house, but he couldn't prevent him from showing up drunk at Ronnie Scott's sometimes. The club owner would take over for him then.

The Danish were also beginning to lose their enthusiasm. His first Copenhagen period had started out full of promise. Shortly after his arrival, he produced three live records in just two days, on January 30 and 31, 1965.[12] The two records he made in September of that year, with Drew/NHØP/Riel and trumpet player Arnved Meyer's Danish mainstream orchestra, were his only official record sessions in two whole years (not counting a brief guest spot with Ellington).[13]

The scandals overshadowed the good concerts. He did play at Ronnie Scott's for a few weeks from late '65 to early '66, where he starred with chanteuse Blossom Dearie. Reviews from this period are uniformly positive.

Webster was beginning to realize that the time had come to move on. His choice fell on the Netherlands, a country he had never been to where his reputation was relatively unsullied (even though news of the Berliner Jazztage fiasco had arrived from neighboring Germany).

In Amsterdam, rents and the cost of living were relatively low. The jazz community was supposed to be as enthusiastic as in Denmark, and Don Byas had been living there since 1955. He had married a Dutch woman, had children, and had been living in Amsterdam for years. He spoke Dutch fairly well—a Dutch accent had even crept into his English. Ben decided to visit the town as a tourist at first, to see if he could get used to the idea of living there.

notes

1 Almost the entire program can be ordered on videotape from the Italian brand Video Collection (ordering number VidJazz 10). The image quality, however, is very poor.

2 From the movie *The Brute and the Beautiful*, by John Jeremy (1989).

3 *Gone With the Wind*, Black Lion (CD), and *Stormy Weather*, Black Lion (CD). According to Yvon Delmarche and Iwan Fresart's discography (*Ben Webster 1931–1973*), Ben made his first European recordings January 14. This is incorrect. The recordings in question (published as a bootleg on *Ben Webster in Europe*, Rarities 45) were made on March 4.

4 *Jazz Hot*, September 6, 1972

5 *At Ease*, Ember CJS 822 (LP). Also: *The Holland Sessions*, Blue Note.

6 *With Steen Vig's Jazz Orchestra*, Storyville.

7 *Ben Webster in London*, Mercury/Fontana.

8 *Ben Webster Meets Bill Coleman*, Black Lion; and Various Artists: *Americans In Europe*, Fontana.

9 *NRC*, November 3, 1965.

10 *Jazzwereld*, March 1966.

11 Jim Godbolt: *All This And Many A Dog*, Quartet Books, 1986.

12 See note 3.

13 *There Is No Greater Love*, Black Lion; *The Jeep Is Jumping*, Black Lion; and Duke Ellington/Ella Fitzgerald: *Ella & Duke at the Côte d'Azur*, Verve.

the amsterdam years

In May 1966, Webster arrived in Amsterdam. Although he had never been very good friends with the hotheaded Byas, it was apparently Byas who helped him find the room at Waalstraat 77, in the upscale Rivierenbuurt in Amsterdam. On the first floor of this house, the Jewish war widow Mrs. Hartlooper supplemented her pension by renting out a small room. Although she had never heard of Ben, she soon ended up spending all her energy pampering and mothering him. Her boarder enjoyed the attention immensely—he had found a substitute for his great-aunt.

A few months after his move, the American journalist Mike Zwerin came to visit him. He described the situation as follows: "Mrs. Hartlooper rented him a room for $20 a week. Webster bought his food and she cooked it. He was her only tenant. While she went into the kitchen, he gulped something stronger than coffee from a flask. 'Know what Hartlooper means?' he asked: 'Fast runner. She is too. Can't keep up with her. Dig—she's 72. Don't know how she does it. Don't know what I'd do without her.' "[1]

Ben Webster was already living in Amsterdam when Dutch journalist Dolf Verspoor wrote a poignant article in the magazine *Jazzwereld*. He praised Webster in the highest terms, deplored his relative neglect by the public, and pointed out that the tenorist had never even played in the Netherlands before. "This artist is now three quarters of an hour away from us by powerboat, in Copenhagen—the time it takes an Amsterdammer to get across town."[2]

When Verspoor realized that the sax great was living within walking distance of his house, he immediately called Michiel de Ruyter, a radio contributor and jazz reviewer for Amsterdam newspaper *Het Parool*. De Ruyter invited Webster over to the studio, and hired a rhythm section consisting of pianist Cees Slinger, bass player Jacques Schols, and drummer John Engels. The three had formerly been members of the Diamond Five, a bop unit that had broken up four years prior to this recording. On June 30, 1966, these musicians first met in the studio for a program called *Studio Acht* (Studio Eight).

Dolf Verspoor went to pick up Webster. "I walked up the stairs, knocked on the door, and found who I expected: a broad-shouldered, heavy man with a friendly face. I introduced myself, and he smiled. We immediately knew that we were going to get along."

Slinger remembers this night clearly, "I came into the studio, and John [Engels] was already there. Ben was straddling a chair with his sax case in his lap, and started testing a reed, 'wooh-wooh.' Two deep sighs. I heard that sound for the first time, and I'll never forget it. What was so special about it? First of all: it was Ben. There he was, the legendary Ben Webster. That was quite impressive in itself, for a couple of simple Dutch boys. These days we are all part of the international scene, but back then we most definitely were not. And that tone... He played two or three notes, and you completely lost it. He was the only one who had that effect on me. That afternoon, we all listened to him with utter adoration."

Bert Vuijsje included the following in arts and politics weekly *Vrij Nederland*: "Thursday night, June 30, he interrupted his vacation (walking, playing billiards, golf) to go make a recording for VARA television station's *Jazz Magazine*. Together with the trio formed by Cees Slinger, Jacques Schols, and John Engels—who were in perfect form that night—he produced one of the most enjoyable studio sessions I have ever witnessed... After about forty

opposite: with his Amsterdam landlady, Mrs. Hartlooper, May 1967

years of making music, he didn't have to develop any new ideas in order to capture the audience. Even if he repeats an existing solo, he pours so much conviction and enthusiasm into it that you find yourself hanging on to his every note, entranced."[3]

Vuijsje ended his article with a recommendation to visit Webster's first big Dutch concert, due to take place on July 13, 1966 in the Amsterdam Concertgebouw—a prestigious concert hall—with Boy Edgar's big band. This concert was part of the Holland Festival, an annual music and theater festival, and excited a lot of expectation.

It turned into a sorry spectacle. "The trouble started during the rehearsal. Jacques Schols' wife had died in a car accident shortly before, so Jacques was completely out of it," de Ruyter recalled. "Ben, in his own way, joined him in his grief. We soon decided that it would be too dangerous to let him descend the stairs at the back of the stage that night, so Ben spent the concert in the front row. Boy pretended not to see him—he sensed the impending disaster—but when the piece was over, Ben unsteadily got to his feet and shouted, 'Now it's my turn.'

"Boy had an orchestra with six trumpets, ten saxophones, trombones and rhythm—altogether about thirty people. Ben started by greeting every single one of them. He slowly moved through the entire group—'Hi, how are you doing?'—until Boy finally got him to the microphone. But now—still during a live broadcast—he started telling the audience all kinds of funny, but disjoined stories.

"The music was nothing special, a little buzzing, some ballad-type things, but Ben just wouldn't stop. In the background, you could suddenly see Boy walking through his orchestra. He gave everyone a note, and created a chord that way—something we always called 'Boy's swimming.'

The piece was in B flat. Ben was really too out of it to carry on. Just when he was about to launch into a new chorus, Boy got up, waved to the orchestra, and made them play a G minor 7th, the parallel chord. Ben whirled around as though he'd been bitten, suddenly unsure of what was going on. Boy grabbed the microphone: 'Ben Webster, ladies and gentlemen, Ben Webster.' "[4]

Some went so far as to dismiss him altogether. The *Elsevier* magazine reviewer, who had not forgotten the Berliner Jazztage calamity, now described him as "Ben Webster, the *former* giant of Hawkins-Hodges caliber," and ended ruefully, "at least the organizers should have known."[5]

So in spite of his resolutions, Webster was sabotaging his chances again. But was he really drunk on stage that often? Acquaintances report that it wasn't that bad, or that frequent. The theory that his benders tended to coincide with large concerts has some merit, as we'll see. Such events usually involved performances by other artists, or endless camera rehearsals, so that he sometimes had to wait half a day before he was on. Long tours were problematic too, especially because the train journeys took so much longer than driving—which he had personally given up—or flying—which he was afraid of. "Far too many planes crash," he used to say.[6] (But for his antipathy to flying, he probably would have visited the States again at least once during his last decade.)

De Ruyter estimates that "about ninety percent of his performances in the Netherlands went fine. He was not an alcoholic in the sense that he couldn't live without alcohol. Sometimes he drank moderately for weeks, just like anybody else. There was always a reason. Meeting old friends, which would make him very emotional. Or one of those television shows where he had to be on hand five hours before the show began."

Hardly any of the Amsterdam witnesses I interviewed had seen him in a truly violent mood. When he had too much to drink he would usually get slow and sleepy, in other cases sentimental and whiney. Rarely did he get verbally aggressive, and the British scene described earlier—when he stalked naked around a hotel brandishing a knife—was unthinkable in his Amsterdam years.

On July 29, 1966, two weeks after the concert with Edgar, he traveled to Juan-les-Pins, France. Norman Granz had invited him over here for a performance with Ellington. The other guests were Ella Fitzgerald and cornettist/violinist/singer Ray Nance, also an Ellington veteran. It turned into a difficult night. Nance was stone drunk, and almost ruined parts of Ella's performance with his random interruptions. Granz: "I went off to the dressing room to pay Ben and Ray. I paid $150 to Ben, which was the agreed fee—excluding expenses—but Ray argued that the deal was $500. That was a lie, but he got very abusive and was shouting about it, so I thought life's too short and I gave him the five hundred and I paid Ben exactly the same."[7]

Webster's performance went without a hitch. He blew a beautiful "All Too Soon," a hit from his first year with Ellington. This was followed by inspired solos in "It Don't Mean A Thing" and "Squeeze Me." The concert was brought out on record shortly afterward. Strangely enough, on the cover Granz only mentioned Webster's contribution to "All Too Soon." Understandably, he chose not to mention Nance at all.[8]

※

In the second half of 1966, Webster began to get settled in Amsterdam. A group of friends was forming around him. With the exception of de Ruyter, who was disabled, his friends would usually meet him at Mrs. Hartlooper's. According to Slinger, his room was definitely no larger than twelve by twelve feet. There was a bed, a writing desk, a small table, two chairs and a linen closet. He could often be found in the living room, which according to Verspoor he had "pleasantly colonized."

He usually worked with Slinger et al., but sometimes played with stand-ins. For instance, on August 21, 1966, he gave a concert with Louis van Dijk on piano, Jacques Schols on bass, and Leo de Ruyter on drums. This concert, in Rotterdam, the Netherlands, was such a success that newspaper *NRC* hailed it as a performance "where he did away with any fatalistic notions of past glory and alcoholism in one fell swoop." The accompaniment's performance was "remarkably solid," and "Webster's final notes in his encore ("Over the

Rainbow") happened to coincide with the bells of the Saint Laurens Church tolling midnight. A worthy conclusion to an admirable concert."[9]

Then there were the tours. In November 1966, he did a series of concerts in London, and played in Copenhagen with Hawkins. Hawkins was on a European tour with JATP at the time, and his appearance must have amazed Webster: the 62-year-old tenor giant now had a wild gray beard, and his clothes hung about his emaciated body. Hawkins was suffering from depression and, though he drank a great deal, hardly ate anything anymore.

Danish television producer Sten Bramsen wanted to seize this opportunity to have them perform one of their 1957 duets together again, "You'd Be So Nice To Come Home To." To Bramsen's surprise, Hawkins said, "I don't know that piece." But after some urging, Bramsen managed to record a decent version after all.[10]

In December 1966, Ben played at Ronnie Scott's for another four weeks. In January 1967, still in England, the first record sessions under his name since 1965 ensued: one with pianist Dick Katz, one with organist Allen Haven.[11] In March, he played in Switzerland with trombonist Vic Dickenson, trumpeter Buck Clayton, and local pianist Henry Chaix.

Back in Amsterdam, he was approached by Johan van der Keuken. This 29-year-old film producer wanted to shoot a short film about Ben's stay in Europe. They became good friends, and their cooperation resulted in the film *Big Ben*. Van der Keuken: "I first met Ben in the winter of '66–'67. Michiel [de Ruyter] had brought us into contact. In March '67, I suggested making a movie about him. We worked on it until June, at great intervals.

"As an introduction, I started recording some conversations with a tape recorder. Suddenly, he got unbelievably distrustful. He retreated into his room, and made me wait in the living room. After a while, he came back to tell me he was willing to continue working together. He later told me that he had thought I wanted to 'steal' his stories. That maybe I wanted to show off with his anecdotes. Out in his room, he began to think that I might be sincere after all. At which he became so touched he started crying. And by the time he came out, I could do no wrong in his eyes."

On Monday, October 16, 1967, *Big Ben* first aired on VPRO TV, at 9:45 PM. The film was generally well received, although some jazz fans objected to its fragmentary character. They would rather have seen a perfectly chronologically structured documentary, with longer musical interludes. But according to the filmmaker, Webster was very pleased with the result. Van der Keuken: "I was a little nervous when I first showed Ben the film. But he said, 'You captured so much of the music...' "

※

In the spring of 1967, plans arose for a new jazz hall. Verspoor, de Ruyter, and several other jazz fans thought it was outrageous that, even though Byas and now Webster had moved to Amsterdam, there was still no decent arena for regular jazz concerts. The Sheherazade, where Cees Slinger's Diamond Five had played for four years, had closed back in 1962.

Verspoor: "There was an artists' society, Arti et Amicitiae [Latin meaning "For Art and Friendship"], which seemed like an interesting venue. It was a very closed society, very intellectual and formal, but we had a friend who was a regular: Steven Kwint, a painter and great Webster admirer. He got a foot in the door for us, which allowed us to organize regular Thursday-night jazz concerts."

On April 8, 1967 "Jazzart" was inaugurated in style by both Webster and Byas. Reporter Martin Schouten covered the event in *Jazzwereld*: "Arti. The club is a huge, dark brown cave. In the back: a bar and two billiards tables. On the street side, some tables, chairs, a small stage and a grand piano... Small and sinewy Byas, large and heavy Webster—they formed an unreal reincarnation of Laurel and Hardy, in black."[12]

According to Schouten, Ben "won" from Byas on the opening night. De Ruyter later said, "Don was a very quick guy of course, just listen to his duet with [bassist] Slam Stewart in "I Got Rhythm" from '45, that was really the high point of his career. Ben could do the same thing, but he was much more into ballads and medium-fast things. Anyway, right at the opening piece, Don grabs the first solo. He goes all over the horn, opens up his whole box of tricks, and when he's finished, he looks at Ben with this look of, 'OK—now your turn.'

"Ben looks at him sidelong for a moment, waits at least two-and-a-half bars, and then just plays fffvvvooo,

Ben in Arti et Amicitiae, May 1967.

fffvvvooo—two magnificent sighs. He then looks at Don again for a moment, and that's when he really starts going. Don had had a bit more to drink that night, so artistically, Ben beat him. I thought that was a very fine moment."[13]

Bert Vuijsje: "Webster usually gave his rival the first solo, let him do his thing, but then resolutely set the musical relations straight: unperturbed, he waited eight measures or so for the applause for Byas' vigorous gymnastics to die down, and then simply started his solo with three serene notes, which definitively established who was the greater musician."[14]

Soon after this memorable occasion, Webster traveled to England, where he did a tour with the rhythm section of the Alex Welsh band and his tenor colleagues Bud Freeman, Eddie Miller, and Eddie "Lockjaw" Davis. Van der Keuken, cameraman as well as director, joined the group, along with sound technician Yvonne Apol, his wife at the time.

In this period he had his sound equipment shipped in from New York, a sign that he was planning an extended stay in Amsterdam. Always interested in sound technique, Webster owned a Bang and Olufsen stereo that was very advanced for the time. He had stored it in New York—possibly with Hinton—for three years.

On May 11, 1967, Byas got his first chance for revenge since their initial duel at Jazzart. *Vrij Nederland* magazine: "He [Byas] dropped his tasteless high shrieking and was generally calmer and more composed, which allowed you to enjoy his rich harmonic variations and robust tone. Webster, who had to play on a borrowed tenor sax, was unable to counter this with his usual masterful performance. He apparently had some trouble with the instrument, and didn't take any risks trying to outdo Byas."[15] He had borrowed the sax from George Johnson, another American living in the Netherlands.

Jazzwereld: "At the end of the evening, Webster challenged Byas to a game of billiards. I don't know how this ended, but [Webster] is second to none when it comes to billiards."[16]

In the following months Webster took it easy. Most of the now numerous summer festivals had not yet started. He played some venues in Holland—seldom more than twice a week—and got the occasional offer from outside the country.

In July, he was a guest at the Finnish Pori Jazz Festival, where he was accompanied by Drew, Ørsted-Pedersen, and drummer Albert "Tootie" Heath, who was living in Copenhagen at the time. He also played at the Norwegian Molde Jazz Festival. His "How Long Has This Been Going On" was described by critic Joachim Ernst Berendt as "the highlight of the whole festival."[17]

⨳

In the fall of 1967, Ben began to entertain more Dutch offers. Among "Ome Ben's" (Uncle Ben's) performances of this period was a date with Slinger, Schols, and Engels, at the Alcuin in Delft on October 14 (for the Novum jazz society). According to newspaper *Het Binnenhof*, Webster got an "enormous ovation" from the Alcuin crowd.[18] Webster usually got a ride home from

Slinger, but this time he chose to stay the night. Whenever he did, he'd take the train home the following morning.

Novum Jazz records show that Ben received a fee of *f*150—the equivalent of $75—plus expenses. His hotel bill, according to the Juliana Hotel in Delft, came to *f*16 for the room, plus another 3.75 for three eggs, a glass of milk and three beers. Tax was *f*2.90 more. That's how it was back in 1967: you phoned Ben Webster at his home, and a few weeks later he would come play at your club for less than $90, expenses included. If you want to get a musician of his stature on a European stage today, you'll easily pay a hundred times that much.

Between all these successful club performances in October 1967, he had one concert in a large hall as well, in the Scheveningen Kurhaus. On October 21, the Nationaal Jazz Concours took place at this venue. Webster was expected to be the high point of the evening again—he headed the only professional formation of the night (not counting the Stork Town Dixie Kids). He was initially supposed to play with Slinger-Schols-Engels, but when it turned out that they were unable to come, the organizer wanted to have him play with Tony Nolte on piano, Koos Serierse on bass, and Han Bennink on drums. The latter two were also going to perform with the Stork Town Dixie Kids that night.

When Webster realized the size of the festival, he asked for a $150 fee. Records show he did receive this, but the performance turned into a disaster that all the media compared to the Berliner Jazztage. He arrived on stage half an hour late, played a few measures from "Our Love Is Here to Stay," and went back to the dressing room to get his hat. He didn't return for a long time, and only returned occasionally to tell some unintelligible stories or blow a handful of notes.

Half the audience left before the show was over—something he was oblivious to. When the organizer was about to have a word with him in the dressing room, Webster said he had enjoyed the concert immensely, and that the trio had really given their all that night.

Even more risky than large concerts were reunions with old colleagues from the States. Such meetings usually began with enthusiastic hugs, followed by a drinking spree where old memories were revived and feelings of nostalgia were revived. Some hours later Ben would have to be dragged home to Mrs. Hartlooper—more often than not physically supported by friends or bystanders.

On October 25, 1967, alto sax player Phil Woods visited him at home. Woods was in the country because he was to play at the Rotterdam Jazz Festival with Thelonious Monk three days later. Tenor saxophonist, car salesman, and jazz journalist Hans Dulfer was present on this Wednesday afternoon as well. After Webster's death, he reported that Webster seemed like a pleasant enough guy in van der Keuken's film, but that in reality he moved around Hartlooper's apartment like "a Saint Bernard in a gazebo."

"Webster got up to call the milkman and order thirty bottles of beer, and swept three geraniums to the floor with his bathrobe without even noticing, rested his head next to, instead of against, the doily on the armchair, and burped so loudly that the neighbors three floors up could probably hear it.

"The latest news and gossip had been exchanged, and nostalgia was beginning to get the upper hand by the time the milkman arrived and put down the thirty beers, trying in vain to get his money out of him...

"Webster then told Woods how he discovered Charlie Parker and, in spite of Johnny Hodges' protests, took him into his band. 'Nobody wanted to let him play with us, not even Ellington. But I saw how talented he was right from the start!'

"After the milkman had come by a third time, and widow Hartlooper had come home—for some reason she was not the least bit upset about the mess—Ben got a little melodramatic. Just as in his solos, he suddenly returned to the beginning. 'My mother,' he sobbed, 'how I wish I could see her again just once.'

"It didn't take long before Phil Woods was dragged along by Ben, and started getting his own misery off his chest... The evening (which it has become by now) ended with the mess these meetings generally turned into during Ben's final years."[19]

※

In November of 1967, Webster and Byas lost their beloved meeting place in Amsterdam; Jazzart was suspended for lack of funds. The final concert took place on November 16.

In December '67 and January '68, Webster played in the U.K. He visited Hawkins again, who was working at Ronnie Scott's. Webster got up on stage next to him a few times, but Hawkins did not appreciate it. Why did Hawkins, unlike Ben, never allow guests to join in? "Ben needs them—I don't" was his standard reply. Hawkins had become even thinner, and continued to act stranger and less accessible all the time.

The English trumpeter Humphrey Lyttelton remembered that an aristocratic couple once asked Ben to introduce them to Hawkins. "Ben Webster duly obliged, the couple sat down next to Hawkins, and there descended upon the little group a fathomless and seemingly eternal silence." Another night, Webster went to visit Hawkins in his dressing room at Ronnie Scott's. He was happy to see Hawk and started telling all kinds of stories. The only reply Hawk mumbled was "yep, yep" and "uh-huh."[20]

On January 17, 1968, a concert was scheduled for the two at the University of Reading, a small town near London. At this point, Hawkins' life style—a lot of alcohol, virtually no food—was definitely taking its toll. He wanted the concert to go ahead no matter what, but had to be carried off the stage after a few choruses. It later turned out he had caught pneumonia. Webster was in good form, and took care of the rest of the evening. Incidentally, Hawkins ignored all medical advice and went on a tour of Scandinavia in February. He died on May 19, 1969.

When Hawkins' engagement at Ronnie Scott's ended in

January 1968, Webster took over. He was accompanied by, among others, Stan Tracey on piano and Tony Crombie on drums. Derek Jewell for the *Sunday Times*: "He does not now seem to push himself in search of new ideas as hard as Hawk; nor does he take so many chances." But, he added, "His tone was silkier, dreamier, sexier than Hawkins'."[21]

The number of record sessions was very limited at this stage—most Dutch firms didn't even seem to know that he was living in Amsterdam. His last official recording in Holland dates from April 1967. On January 1 and 2, 1968, German critic/producer Joachim Ernst Berendt brought him and Byas over to a studio in the southern German town of Villingen.[22] The session wasn't successful, though Berendt in the liner notes does his best to convince the listener otherwise.

De Ruyter: "That record? Disgraceful! They were both drunk as skunks and produced nothing at all. A worthless record." Egbert de Bloeme had this to say about it: "Byas had a very high opinion of himself. And he was a star soloist of course, but whenever Ben was around, he never realized he had to be a bit more modest. And if you added alcohol to this mixture, they would both get pretty irritable. Ben later told me that he refused to play together with Byas after a few pieces. They each recorded an additional short solo piece, and that was that."

Webster was not doing too well these days as it was. In the car with Berendt, on the way to the studio, he'd wondered aloud several times, "Where should I go live?" He had spent a lot of money getting his sound installation shipped in from New York, and was pampered by his landlady to his heart's content, but something was bothering him.

The reason he had come to Europe was to get more work and more respect. Respect he enjoyed, but work remained scarce. In Europe, he took part in one, two, maybe three official record sessions a year—almost nothing, compared to his earlier routine. And the initial excitement about his presence in the Netherlands had subsided.

Fortunately, some live recordings were brought out on record posthumously. This included a recording made with Drew, NHØP, and Albert Heath for Danish radio on March 6, 1968 and in the summer of that year.[23] On April 8, 1968, he performed for Dutch radio with Byas, Slinger, Langereis, and Ypma. Someone recorded this radio concert, and several pieces were released by bootleg record label Rarities—described as "Scandinavian recordings" with, incredibly, "unknown accompanying artists"![24]

In September 1968, he toured Europe with some old friends, including trumpet player Bill Coleman and tenorist Buddy Tate. The drummer on the tour was Wally Bishop, a musician of his generation who had been living in Holland since 1951, but whom—strangely enough—he seldom played with.

In 1968, Ben was involved in a Dutch movie for the second time. Director Bob Rooyens was making a film about the Boy Edgar Big Band, starring Webster, singer Betty Carter, and trumpeter Maynard Ferguson. The program lasted fifty minutes, and was entitled *Sessie*.

The movie consisted of recording scenes for a fictitious record, full of discussions and small conflicts. Edgar: "If we were really trying to make a record, we wouldn't have been blathering on like that of course. My intent was mostly to get people to open up." They filmed non-stop for twenty-four hours, and still Edgar complained afterward, "Just one more hour and we could have made a great recording."[25]

The film was broadcast on October 1, 1968. Dutch humorist Simon Carmiggelt saw the program, and devoted a column to it, which he titled *Lover Man*.

"You saw a careful registration of what happens when Boy Edgar's Big Band goes into the studio to make a record. It was a wonderful sight. All of Holland's big jazz boys were brought together in that quasi-frivolous musicians' atmosphere, all hoping things would come together. At some point, Edgar said, 'Guys, now it's Ben's turn. But let's see how Ben is doing today...' Because that was unpredictable, with a man who led a difficult life like Ben. He entered, dressed completely in black, like he was going to a funeral. He didn't say a word. He took his instrument to his lips. And while everyone listened in tense expectation, he played "Lover Man."

"I'd never heard it played more beautifully. You could see the others get an expression that conveyed, 'Ben's doing well today.' "

About a week after the program aired, Carmiggelt and Webster met at Amsterdam Central Station. "Between all these travelers getting off the train, there was Ben

Webster, with his big instrument in a case. He was wearing a frilly red shirt and moved with a tired, heavy man's gait. How lonely he looked, walking down the tunnel on the way to the exit. I hastened my step and said to him, in my best English, 'Mr. Webster, I thought your "Lover Man" on TV was fantastic.' I really startled him and he looked at me, astonished, leaning his back against the wall. 'Oh—thank you,' he said, with a faint smile. I stood before him for a moment longer, not sure what to do. Then I just moved on, with the feeling I really shouldn't have done that. Or should I have? When I looked back, I saw he was staring after me, looking dismayed. My wife said, 'It's probably because of that raincoat of yours. He probably thought you were a detective or something.' Oh well. Still, I've never heard a better version of "Lover Man"."

Unfortunately, Carmiggelt made a minor mistake. Ben didn't play "Lover Man" in the movie, but "The Man I Love."

※

In September 1968, almost a year after the end of Jazzart, things finally livened up in the Amsterdam jazz world. Hans Dulfer organized a series of concerts in Paradiso, a former church in the center of the city, which had been made over into a hippie center.

Dulfer realized that Jazzart's downfall had been its obscurity, and he didn't want to fall into the same trap. Public relations was one of his strong points, so that was no problem at all. Early October, he sent out about 750 invitations: "Wednesday night, October 26, is going to be a memorable evening for an imported Amsterdammer. That is the night when the committee for Your Jazz in Paradiso [by which he meant himself] has organized an evening around the most impressive and soulful Waalstraat inhabitant, Uncle Ben; also known in jazz chronicles as BEN WEBSTER (The Giant Of The Tenor Sax)." He was to play with Slinger, Langereis, and Bennink.

Bert Vuijsje wrote the following in *Jazzwereld*: "Webster was clearly into it, and he was even more adventurous than I have ever heard him play in Holland (daring runs and passionate honks in a fast tempo; Hodges-like glissandos and vibratos in the ballads)." And Bennink "excelled with a performance that was rock solid yet quick to respond."[26]

Chemist and jazz journalist Tom Beetz, a student in Amsterdam at the time, seemed to remember that Webster could be found in Paradiso almost every Wednesday night. "He'd always come staggering in toward the end of the concert. He was usually at least somewhat tipsy, and planning to get good and drunk. He'd take a seat at the bar with his saxophone case, and right away someone would ask him, 'Are you gonna play? Come on, please?' And Ben would mutter something like 'No man, I'm tired, man.' But during the final number, he'd get up on stage after all. He would walk up the steps, Hans Dulfer quickly pulled up a chair, and at his leisure, almost in slow motion, he started assembling his sax. That took forever. You'd think—he's never going to make it, the piece will be over before he's through.

But he always made it. He didn't play with any of the avant-garde groups of course, but with people like Piet Noordijk, J.R. Monterose, who was out here all the time, Lucky Thompson, Dexter Gordon, and so on."

⁂

On January 12, 1969, when Webster had been living in Amsterdam for two-and-a-half years, he first entered a Dutch recording studio. The result was far from satisfactory; he was not there with Slinger et al., but with three amateurs from the north: pianist Frans Wieringa, bass player Gerard Holgreve, and drummer Tom van Steenderen. A reliable witness of this occasion was Rein de Graaff, a northern pianist of quite a different caliber.

De Graaff: "Everything had been arranged by and for the benefit of Frans Wieringa, a young guy in his 20s. He wanted to make a name for himself as a musician because he could play the piano a little, copied some Oscar Peterson stuff. Then he got the idea to make a record with his amateur group, and why not go ahead and ask Ben Webster. He offered him a nice sum of money so Webster must have thought, 'A gig is a gig.' "[27]

Just six weeks later, the album—entitled *At Ease*—hit the stores; shortly thereafter it was even reissued by the English label Ember. The review in *Jazzwereld* was crushing: "After six exhausting hours, in which Webster mainly had to give the others jazz lessons, barely 35 minutes of music was recorded, which...barely reached minimal professional standards." And, "It is a disgrace that this record was ever issued at all."[28]

A welcome improvement over *At Ease* is *Live in*

Amsterdam, a registration of an excellent concert that took place on January 24, 1969, but wasn't transferred to vinyl until 1989. This concert—with Slinger, Langereis and Ypma—took place at the Amsterdam Lurelei Theater, and was recorded by Egbert de Bloeme, without commercial objectives.[29]

Shortly after this performance, Webster got a chance to meet up with some old colleagues. In March, he played in Belgium with artists that included alto player Eddie "Cleanhead" Vinson, pianist Jay McShann, and bass player Gene Ramey. Upon his return to Amsterdam, the tour's stress caught up with him, and he fell ill with the Mao flu. On March 23, 1969, under a pile of blankets, he was interviewed by a journalist from the daily newspaper *Nieuws van de Dag*.

The occasion for the interview was his 60th birthday, which was going to be celebrated in Paradiso on the night of March 26 to 27. "The atmosphere there is great," the tenorist assured him. He promised he would be there, no matter how he felt. He muttered something about his "good times" with Ellington, lit yet another cigarette, and fell to musing about the past.

A few days before, "The Committee" (i.e. Dulfer) had circulated a very formal invitation: "Benjamin Francis Webster, man and artist, will reach the youthful age of sixty this Wednesday. To celebrate this momentous occasion, a festive gathering will take place on Wednesday night [March 26] in Paradiso. The artist, accompanied by a highly accomplished rhythm section, will perform a number of favorites from his repertory.

"We deemed it appropriate to further enhance the evening's festive character by asking a woman for a performance for the first time: singer Ann Burton. After midnight, there will be an opportunity to congratulate the artist also known as 'the king of the tenor saxophone' at the bar, and to bestow upon him any tokens of appreciation."

Ben had asked Dulfer to invite Ann Burton (1933–1989; real name, Anna Rafalowics). Her nascent career was already stalled, and he was trying to rekindle interest in her. Dulfer went to a novelty store with Martin Schouten and honored Dutch tradition by purchasing bunting, and cardboard cutouts that read "Long Live The Birthday Boy" and the number 60. He also arranged for an enormous birthday cake with a saxophone and sixty candles. Initially, Langereis and Bennink were going to play with Slinger, but at the last moment the members of Slinger's regular trio, Schols and Engels, turned out to be available.

That night broke a record by Paradiso standards with 1,500 guests; at 10:30, the fire brigade forced the venue to turn back a hundred more hopefuls. "Uncle Ben" was not prepared for such a crush. Newspaper *Algemeen Handelsblad*: "He looked a little taken aback when at nine-fifteen he ascended the stage, and announced that he was ready to start his next sixty years."

He kept his solos fairly brief at first—the flu was taking its toll. One unannounced person, added at his request, was trumpet player of the Dutch Swing College Band Ray Kaart, "an excellent player in the thundering

Eldridge idiom."

After a set by Ann Burton it was Ben's turn again, who "with a rare sense of timing managed to finish a piece precisely at midnight, while Dulfer—someone who also knows about timing—carried an enormous birthday cake onto the stage at the same time, while yet someone else started the Dutch birthday song of "Long Shall He Live," which was immediately taken up by the entire audience... At which a deeply touched Ben Webster blew out all sixty candles in one mighty breath." Then followed presents and flowers, not just for Ben, but for Mrs. Hartlooper as well.

The climax of the evening was the final set, where American musicians Marty Morell (drums) and Eddie Gomez (bass), who had played in a Dutch radio studio earlier that night, took over from Schols and Engels. The tenor player got Burton and Kaart on the stage, and all of a sudden his flu seemed to have been cured. "He paced through the chords with enormous, bellowing notes, filled the room with his best raw, heartrending blues sound, and even the imperturbable, gum-chewing Morell sat up and took note. That was at one-thirty, when half the audience had already left. But that's the way it goes, that's after-hours work."[30]

According to Dulfer, Webster was a little suspicious at first. "Three times I had to assure him that he really would get paid, in spite of the night's festive character. But once he gets up on the big stage and, after a brief, inaudible conversation with Cees Slinger, launches into "In A Mellow Tone," something changes.

"His sound alone is enough to create a special atmosphere in the hall. His insecurity vanishes instantly, and after he has played a number of fantastic standard choruses, a hand signal that would have befitted the emperor Nero indicates that one of the other musicians may now take a solo.

"Ben meanwhile starts his second act, which is to say that he pulls up the legs of his pants a little, shifts his chair three times, and just before he starts trading the fours with drummer John Engels, he impressively rolls his eyeballs until only the whites are visible. Even the so-called indeterminate endings to his pieces are classics, culminating in a masterful low B flat you can't even hear.

"The end of the set was Ben's own "Cotton Tail," and although physically he's no longer able to reproduce the stunning JATP versions of this piece, and though the Ellington version will never be surpassed, this is Ben at his best. Each lick is his own invention, and nobody will ever be able to improve on his growling choruses...

"With difficulty, he descends the stage via the rickety stairs, to a thundering ovation. When someone offers him a large glass of beer while he is regaining his breath, he resolutely declines. 'I don't want to get drunk at my own party, and by the way, I have decided to stay sober the next sixty years!' Too bad he couldn't keep that resolution."[31]

※

Despite this warm reception, Webster stayed in Amsterdam only two more months. In April 1969 he

went to Copenhagen for a few weeks, where there was more work in studios—he was often invited on radio programs there—as well as in clubs. Several other American expatriates had taken up residence there; he liked playing with Albert Heath and Kenny Drew. Dexter Gordon had also relocated to the city.

On April 20 and 21, he worked with Arnved Meyer's Danish band again. A second guest on this occasion was trumpeter Buck Clayton. The reunion with Clayton can't have been very enjoyable for Webster, because the trumpet player suffered from severe embouchure trouble. An ill-fitting bridge had caused a cut in his upper lip.

Clayton drank large amounts of whisky to dull the pain, a remedy that didn't improve his performance much. A few years later, he gave up the trumpet, and after a few years of office work, he started a new career as arranger and orchestra leader.

By now, *At Ease* had been issued. This monstrosity caused some indignation, and record company Bovema decided to even the score through a session with professional musicians: none other than Slingers–Schols–Engels. The company also wanted to put some thought into the repertoire. Bovema thought it would be a good idea to make this a tribute to Ellington. Dutch jazz aficionado Fred Dubiez, an engineer by trade, was asked to collect some pieces.

Dubiez: "I was especially looking for pieces with a strong melody. Some pieces sound fine with that big Ellington orchestra, but lose their character when they

opposite: Ben's fellow tenor saxophonists Coleman Hawkins (left) and Don Byas

are performed by a quartet. My selection wasn't ready when I found out the session would be pushed forward because Ben was suddenly moving to Copenhagen. The recording was organized in great haste, and Cees Slinger and Ben Webster ended up quickly deciding what to play."

For The Guv'nor is the only acceptable recording Webster made during his three-year stay in Amsterdam, not counting some live recordings that were issued much later. More about this to come.[32]

At the beginning of June, he moved to Copenhagen. The immediate occasion was a studio gig; but, as mentioned earlier, there were contributing factors.

Johan van der Keuken recalled: "There was more work out there, he had a few contacts there, and so he wanted to give Copenhagen a try. The most important reason was that Mrs. Hartlooper was no longer capable of taking care of him, however much she loved him. He had that drinking problem that returned on a regular basis. He got very homesick, especially when he had had a few drinks, so he'd end up making calls to Los Angeles in the middle of the night. And the next morning he wouldn't remember a thing. So his landlady got stuck with these huge telephone bills. She told him it was time for him to start looking for a different place to live. Ben used people *up*. He was surrounded by a small group of people that continued helping him, but eventually it became almost impossible for them to maintain it."

Rens Kwint, one of his core friends: "When Ben finally

realized that he couldn't stay at Mrs. Hartlooper's, he couldn't find a place. We helped him search, but we couldn't find anything in the city because he couldn't prove that he had a regular source of income. Then, Dexter Gordon told him there might be an apartment for him in Copenhagen."

In that same period, Byas too experienced a certain restlessness in overly quiet Amsterdam. An *Esquire* journalist had asked him in 1968 whether he would ever return to the United States. "Maybe just once," was his answer. "One more big tour, and then I'll lay down and die." In July of 1970 he played at the Newport Jazz Festival—his first visit to the United States in almost a quarter of a century. The year after, he toured Japan with Art Blakey's Jazz Messengers.

The reception was not what Byas had imagined, so he returned to Amsterdam where, on August 24, 1972, age 59, he died of throat cancer. He left his wife Jopie with four young children: Dotty Mae, Ellie Mae, Carlotta and Carlos Junior. There are still several entries with his last name in the Amsterdam phone book.

notes

1 *Holland Herald*, 1986.
2 *Jazzwereld*, September 1966.
3 *Vrij Nederland*, July 9, 1966.
4 Michiel de Ruyter and Frank van Dixhoon, *Michiele de Ruyter, Een Leven met Jazz* (Van Gennep 1984).
5 *Elsevier*, July 23, 1966.
6 Cover text to the album *Ben Webster Meets Don Byas*, MPS.
7 Derek Jewell: *A Portrait of Duke Ellington* (Pavillion Books 1986).

8 Duke Ellingon/Ella Fitzgerald: *Ella & Duke at the Côte d'Azur*, Verve.
9 *NRC*, August 23, 1966.
10 John Chilton: *Song of the Hawk* (Quartet Books 1990).
11 Both sessions can be found on *Ben Webster in London*, Mercury/Fontana.
12 *Jazzwereld*, July/August 1967.
13 See note 4.
14 *Vrij Nederland*, April 1967.
15 *Vrij Nederland*, May 1967.
16 *Jazzwereld*, July/August 1967.
17 See note 6.
18 *Het Binnenhof*, October 16, 1980.
19 Hans Dulfer: *Jazz in China* (Bert Bakker 1980).
20 John Chilton: *Song of the Hawk* (Quartet Books 1990).
21 *The Sunday Times*, January 7, 1968.
22 *Ben Webster Meets Don Byas*, MPS.
23 *Plays Ballads*, Storyville, and *Plays Duke Ellington*, Storyville.
24 *Ben Webster in Europe, vol. 2*, Rarities 55 (LP). The pieces are "You'd Be So Nice To Come Home To" and "I Got Rhythm."
25 *De Volkskrant*, October 1, 1968.
26 *Jazzwereld*, December 1968.
27 *At Ease*, Ember CJS 822 (LP). Also: *The Holland Sessions*, Blue Note.
28 *Jazzwereld*, April/May 1969.
29 *Live in Amsterdam*, Affinity.
30 *Algemeen Handelsblad*, March 27, 1969.
31 Hans Dulfer: *Jazz in China* (Bert Bakker 1980).
32 *For the Guv'nor*, Affinity.

someone to watch over me

Egbert de Bloeme: "Waalstraat 77, second floor. I've been there countless times, I'll never forget the place. You went through the front door, and a flight of stairs started right behind the door. He'd usually be sitting on the second floor, behind the lace curtains, so he'd see you coming. You'd wave at him, and you wouldn't even have to ring the bell, because he pulled on a rope upstairs and the front door would swing wide open.

"It was a walk-up apartment in the upscale Rivierenbuurt, where Ben had his own room. There was a piano—he had taken care of that—and everything revolved around him. Mrs. Hartlooper only cooked the way he liked it. Not one but two pork chops, cooked according to his instructions. When he came over for dinner with us, we would always cook him soul food, with beans and such—he loved that.

"He could play all his records and tapes there. He got up around eleven, and then he'd listen to his 'Wakin' Up Music.' This was a tape he had made with all his favorites from his record collection. That tape was always playing while he drank his first cup of coffee with hot milk, which Mrs. Hartlooper always made him. He would sit at the dining room table, still in his pajamas, bathrobe and slippers.

"After his morning coffee, he needed at least another half hour to wash and get dressed. When that was finished he returned to the living room, in a cloud of aftershave. His landlady would usually bring him a second cup of coffee and three eggs, sunny side up, on toast with ham or bacon. She always asked him in Dutch if he liked it, and he would reply, 'Good for the *buik*,' which is Dutch for his huge belly, which he gave a contented pat to while he said that. After breakfast, he would generally spend some time at the piano, and then it was about time for his first bottle of beer.

"Although he was always involved with music, he rarely played the saxophone at home, and definitely not when he had visitors. He would sometimes warm up a little if he hadn't played for a week, but that was all."

Cees Slinger: "There was a very steep, narrow staircase he had to descend with that heavy body of his, while I carried his sax case. And at night, he had to climb back up those stairs again. That was even harder. Mrs. Hartlooper would buy him a present sometimes. I remember she bought him a shirt one time. That was lying on the coffee table in the living room and he was looking at it, saying 'Oh, nice, nice.' "

Ben didn't have many possessions. Besides his saxophone and the piano, he owned about twenty records, a few tapes, and a stereo system. He also had some pictures of the women who raised him, and of the house where he was born.

He once allowed Egbert to copy his Wakin' Up Music tape, on the condition that he would return it the same day. Ben had written "Wakin' Up Music" on the box in his angular handwriting, with a big black felt-tip pen. The tape started with two pieces Art Tatum had recorded for Decca with singer Big Joe Turner: "Wee Baby Blues" and "Corinna Corinna."

It also contained "Someone To Watch Over Me" and "Too Marvelous For Words" played by Art Tatum, "The Joint Is Jumping" and "Handful Of Keys" by Fats Waller, plus four Donald Lambert arrangements of European classical themes: "Elegie," "Anitra's Dance," "Pilgrim's Chorus," and "Sextette." Ben used to be a good friend of Lambert's, a stride pianist who had slipped into obscurity after his New York work in the twenties and thirties. Almost all these pieces had been recorded in 1941.

Johan van der Keuken: "You'd go over in the afternoon, and then you sat at the table in the living room for a few hours, each with a beer in your hand. Even when he was 'not drinking,' he always had a glass in his hand. I think he drank around two or three pints of beer per day. He tended to feed himself with beer, and Mrs. Hartlooper had to make sure he ate well. She treated him like a grown son who just won't take care of himself.

"What did we talk about? About current affairs—he took a great interest in those. American politics, the war in Vietnam. He was utterly opposed to it, of course.

Sometimes he'd also talk about movies he had seen. He loved *The Good, the Bad and the Ugly*. And then there was the zoo—animals fascinated him.

"During the day he was very gallant, he really wanted you to have a good time. He played you a record, and would try all kinds of things to make sure you stayed for as long as possible. His skin was peachy then, and he'd be grinning from ear to ear.

"In the mornings he drank milk, and in the afternoons he switched to beer. When he brought out the hard liquor in the evening, his mood would sometimes turn all of a sudden. He'd start acting hurt, whiney. He always said that it wasn't the musicians who profited from music, but others.

"At such moments, I would get the hell out of there. When he went to the bathroom, I'd simply leave. He would just get so heavy-handed, it was too depressing. After a while I only went over in the afternoons. Look, you get selective. You've also got your own life and troubles, and you wouldn't get around to those otherwise.

"And yet Ben was continually trying to contain himself, to make sure he wouldn't degenerate. It took a lot of his energy. A two-week tour was the maximum he could manage. During the third week, tensions would rise and the stress would get the better of him. He'd have a cognac, and that would be that. This danger always hung over him like the sword of Damocles."

Besides beer, Ben also consumed large amounts of cake. Across the street from his apartment on Waalstraat, on number 58, there was a bakery he often patronized. In 1992, the employees could still remember "a fat black guy from America" who played the sax, and who at times came over more than once a week, sometimes daily, to buy fruitcake. He was supposed to have been "addicted" to that fruitcake.

Rens Kwint: "Mrs. Hartlooper looked good for her age, but then she did wear a wig. It was always a pleasure to visit there. When there were a lot of people, Ben would tell stories about his good times in the United States. He could really tell a story, would act out scenes and imitate... It was like he was on stage.

"He once bought a bicycle to get into better shape. He didn't ride it too often, though. When he was in a good mood, he would walk to a butcher several neighborhoods away in the Jordaan, and point out which part of the cow he wanted. He was a cheerful guy on his good days, always trying to make others laugh."

Egbert de Bloeme: "He loved playing billiards. He thought it was interesting that we play billiards so differently from the way it is played in the U.S. He even went to Belgium once to take lessons with billiard champion Ceulemans. He kept talking about 'Cool Man.' I had no idea what he was talking about at first."

Dolf Verspoor: "Ben liked to go out and play billiards somewhere with Don Byas. But he also went into town to do other things. He visited a prostitute sometimes, and then he'd come back, beaming with pride, and tell us how well he could still do that."

Jetske Verspoor: "He never told me things like that. He

was far too prudish for that."

Egbert de Bloeme: "I met him at Jazzart. I was studying law in Amsterdam, I had a car, and could pretty much arrange my time the way I liked it. I spent a lot of time on jazz and on Ben. I went along to a lot of concerts, because I took care of transportation. Ben probably didn't have a driver's license anymore—I never asked him about it. He thought it was pretty convenient, an Amsterdam friend with a car. These things can get annoying after a while, but that wasn't the case with him.

"He mostly talked about fellow musicians, and they were always positive stories. He was afraid to tell certain things. He had grown up in cities where nightlife was largely in the hands of the underworld, and certain things were best not spoken about. He was afraid to do so even all these years later, in Amsterdam. You'd sometimes notice that he had crossed the line—in his opinion anyway—and then he'd say, 'I'd better not go into this subject any further.'

"[Singer] Babs Gonzales was different. The man stayed with us for a while. Ben came over sometimes, and the two would be having a heated conversation. I sometimes taped those conversations, which terrified Ben. Babs always had wild stories, about an alleged affair between Quincy Jones and Dinah Washington, things like that. Ben always tried to shut him up. Because when he knew the tape was rolling, he'd be sweating with terror. Just imagine if this came out!

"The idea never left him that someone might be listen-

opposite: in Amsterdam, 1968

ing, anywhere. As a black man in the United States, he had learned that there were certain things you just didn't talk about. When someone had done something to him that he didn't like—and that must have happened on occasion—he kept quiet about it. He complained sometimes, but never gave any details."

Michiel de Ruyter: "Ben never talked to me about black and white. I heard him talk in a low tone to Don Byas once about tours in the American South. But when I came closer, the conversation stopped."

Cees Slinger: "He didn't have a manager. The groups he played with were usually formed by the person who was first approached. I think we, as accompanying artists, got around $50 to $75 per night. Normal work, gigs in clubs. Ben got more, I think around $150 to $250. And that was about right, I thought."

Egbert de Bloeme: "At Jazzart he earned at least $175. The Lurelei concert that was issued later I remember distinctly: $250.[1] I would pay the accompanists at least $100 each. Those were princely sums at the time. I wanted to pay musicians what I felt they deserved. That's why I could only book small groups.

"He could be a little naive when it came to business. You'd think that all those years in the business would have been education enough, but he hadn't learned anything. He kept letting people take advantage of him, and it was his own fault really. He always trusted these quick agreements made over the phone.

"Take for instance that record with Ellington pieces, *For the Guv'nor*. Ben asked for a thousand dollars for that session. And royalties, of course. He always thought in dollars. He always asked for a dollar fee when you discussed gigs. It was fine to calculate how much that was in Dutch guilders and pay him that, but he never stopped thinking in dollars. That gave him a sense of stability.[2]

"And those thousand dollars, after the job was done, had suddenly turned into a thousand guilders [worth half as much]. That made him really mad. But he had no written contract, they had simply closed the deal over the phone. That's not a way to get rich of course. He led a fairly expensive lifestyle too, with all that booze and cabs everywhere. When you saw how much he spent and how often he played, there can't be much left at the end of the day.

"The concerts at Lurelei didn't start until late at night—there was a cabaret performance in that hall first. I had to keep an eye on Ben on nights like that, or he would be exhausted by the time he had to play. So when he had to play in Lurelei, I spent the entire day with him. I got him over to my house, and we would play records, look at pictures and talk.

"Then we would go out to dinner, and drove to the theater. He would still be in great shape, and that's why I managed to make such an excellent recording there.[3] I would take him home afterwards, or he would take a taxi. The cab dropped him off at the front door and he usually managed to make his way up the stairs. There was one time when we had to drag him up the stairs. With three people: the cab driver, my wife, and I.

Because the guy weighed a ton. He was stone drunk, but sooner or later he had to get to bed. So we tucked him in nicely."

Ronnie Scott: "I remember we did a gig in Barnes. I would play for half an hour, announce Ben, and then I'd be gone and he would be on for the rest of the night, with the same rhythm section. When I had to start, he still hadn't arrived. I played for an hour, and then he finally showed up. You could always tell when Ben was over-refreshed, because he had one of those hand-painted American ties with a nude girl on it. And when he was drunk, he had the shirt open at the neck, with the tie just hanging down, not done up.
"He came into the hall and said:
'Stick around for a while and play with me.'
'Okay.'
'What do you want to play?'
'Perdido.'
'Great.'
"And he beat it in: 'One... two... three... four [very slow tempo].' And we played "Perdido" in that tempo, for twenty minutes. And then followed "Danny Boy," which was a work of art when he was sober. But the way he played it now, any Irishman would have shot him on the spot."[4]

※

Rens Kwint: "One time he got really aggressive. That was at a concert with Dexter Gordon in Beverwijk. He grabbed his saxophone and refused to play any more. I was in the back of the room, talking to some people at the bar, and he yelled, 'Get your hand off her knees!' Even though those guys weren't touching me at all—I was just talking to them.

"And when we—Steven, Dexter, Ben, and I—left in the car, he just wouldn't stop bellyaching about Dexter, that he was weak because he used drugs and couldn't play otherwise. Dexter felt embarrassed, because he saw Ben as the great master. And whenever Dexter very carefully tried to say anything, Ben yelled, 'Don't shout in front of a lady!' While Ben was doing nothing but shout. That's when we got a glimpse of what Ben could also be like."

Dolf Verspoor: "One time, he was invited to go on a tour to Warsaw. He was away for about ten days. On the day of his return, I went over to visit him. He lay on his bed, completely worn out. Mrs. Hartlooper told me that the cab driver had dragged him up the stairs the night before. I sat down next to his bed, and he slowly reconstructed the experience.

"He had seen the poverty, the oppression in Poland. All those poor, terrified people, who saw him as a representative of the free West. He had spent an eternity on the train at the borders between East and West Germany, and between East Germany and Poland.

"Everything he earned there he gave back to his Polish accompanists, and he returned with his sax and a few bottles of Polish vodka. Over the course of that endless train trip he drank them all—there was just a splash left in one bottle. He was so shocked that it took months before he could talk about it at all."

Cees Slinger: "We had a relationship of trust. When I

picked him up and he sat down next to me in my car, he would sometimes say, 'Why don't you hang on to this.' And he'd give me his hip flask, and left me in charge of rationing his alcohol. And when I said, 'Ben, you've had enough,' he accepted that. But sometimes others bought him so many drinks that the system broke down altogether.

"I spent one night with him that I'll never forget. That night was just one disaster after another. We had a concert with Boy Edgar, in Oostende, Belgium. We took the whole orchestra over there in a bus, with Ben as guest soloist. I think we played reasonably well. But there was no money. Damn it, there was no money. Ben had had quite a few drinks that night, and he also brought a bottle onto the bus. On the way back, he started attacking just about everyone on the bus, along the lines of, 'You, caucasians, you, caucasians! You are letting me down, and you haven't arranged things right,' and so on and so forth.

"To make matters even worse, the bus ran out of diesel on the way back. [Tenor sax player] Rudi Brink and I went to find a gas station, which took us hours and hours on foot, and we got a jerrycan full of diesel. Everybody was pissed off that there wasn't any money—nobody had received any, nor has anyone ever seen a penny from that concert. Boy had simply not made the right arrangements. That night Ben felt deeply unhappy, he had had a lot to drink, and old hurt suddenly reared its head."

※

Johan van der Keuken: "Ben had fairly conventional ideas about music. In those days, I was crazy about Archie Shepp. I noticed that Shepp drew in part on Ben's tradition. I once brought over a Shepp record that contained Ellington's "In a Sentimental Mood." I started playing it and after three notes, Ben said, 'Stop!' He walked to the back, to his room, and came back with his saxophone—something that had never ever happened, he never touched the thing at home—and said, 'Play that record again, will you.'

"I played it, and right after the first note, he said, 'Stop!' He took his sax and played that first note. 'That's how you're supposed to play that.' One note! 'That kid is crazy.' Then he put his tenor away again. He was through with Shepp. From Ben's perspective, he was right of course—it was Ellington material, and that was holy. Ben knew exactly how Ellington would have wanted to hear it played."

In 1973, Webster said, "I've no time for some of the guys playing this new thing. They just run up and down the scale making all the noises they can think of on the saxophone. They have no respect for tone or execution or anything like that. They don't know the horn. One guy I thought was really trying was John Coltrane. He had a method, a real system, y'know. I liked to hear Coltrane."[5]

Cees Slinger: "In a musical sense, he was easy to work with. He always played the same pieces and once you knew those, you were set. He didn't exactly have precise timing. He wove through everything, but it always matched up at the end. He had his own timing, which was very laid back. Sometimes he fell behind considerably, but he somehow managed to make it sound good. I didn't always agree with the chords he wanted to hear. He sometimes played something on the piano that he wanted to hear, and I'd think, 'I would have done that differently.'

"Ben did allow you to make some bebop changes, he had no problem with that. He didn't follow you exactly, but it still sounded great. Ben played melodically. It was no use trying to analyze what notes he played in relation to the chords. You can do that with Charlie Parker. Like Jimmy Knepper, Ben draped his melodies over the chords, and it always worked."

Rens Kwint: "Steven first met Ben at Arti et Amicitiae. Although they couldn't communicate very well at first—Steven's English was limited—they understood each other completely. They were both large, somewhat naive men who lived solely for their work, and everything else came second. They shared a certain discontentment. Steven too had the feeling that his talent wasn't fully appreciated. Steven invited Ben over to his studio a few times, and made two portraits of him. That's how they became good friends.

"They spent a lot of time together. We had a house on the Stadhouderskade. Steven's studio was at the other end of the city center, on the Brouwersgracht, and Ben often came over to sit around and play a little saxophone while Steven was painting. And every once in a while they'd have a beer and wander around the neigh-

 opposite: with Steven Kwint, at Kwint's studio, 1968.

borhood some. They didn't talk much. They eventually ended up walking all the way over to our house for dinner. Or we went out to find him a billiards table somewhere."

Considering the closeness to his mother and great-aunt, his emotional attachment to men like Kwint, Blanton, *et al.*, the swift dissolution of his marriage and the paucity of romantic relationships overall, as well as the idealized image he had of women—considering all this, some people have wondered whether Webster might have been gay or bisexual. Whatever his proclivities, there is no evidence he had erotic relationships with men, and if he was closeted, he may have been hardly aware of it himself, so intent was he from an early age to cease being the "sissy with the violin" and develop into an accepted member of the jazz fraternity.

Dolf Verspoor: "Steven was really one with Ben; they were just like twin brothers. He identified completely with Ben. He was a farmer's son who didn't speak anything other than Dutch, but who had been blessed with artistic gifts. Almost all the English Steven knew he learned from Ben, so he mainly knew musicians' jargon, with a Kansas City accent.

"Toward the end, Ben limited his repertory. He started playing more ballads. One of his favorite pieces was "Someone To Watch Over Me." That could have been his motto. He always needed someone to watch over him. There was a whole circle of friends around him. Friends who would call each other up to say, 'How is Ben doing, could you go over and have a look, Egbert has already tried.' And then it would turn out he had the flu, or too much to drink the night before.

"You didn't mind doing it for him, and you realized he was getting on in years. *Someone To Watch Over Me.* Raised by women, never had a father, and what he felt as a loss, he wanted to give to others. With his music and his presence.

"His music had special meaning for me. I had a daughter who had a heart problem, and who only lived for eighteen months. That affected me deeply. She died shortly before Ben moved to Amsterdam. I was attached to his music as it was, but after that, I couldn't do without. It's thanks to his records that I made it through that period. I later told him that. When my next daughter was born, he was so moved that he kept sending flowers and postcards. He felt a really strong connection."

Jetske Verspoor remembers one of their final meetings. "There was a party with Dexter Gordon and Ben. They were both out here on tour. There was dancing as well. Ben was much too overweight for that. He just quietly leaned back in an easy chair, talking to Dolf. I had been dancing for a while, and then I sat down next to Ben. Dolf was on his other side. When Dolf got up to get a drink, Ben leaned over to me, looked at me with that gentle look in his eyes and said earnestly, 'Be good to your man.' "

notes

1 *Live in Amsterdam*, Affinity.
2 *For the Guv'nor*, Affinity.
3 See note 1.
4 From the movie *The Brute and the Beautiful* by John Jeremy (1989).
5 *Jazz Journal*, 1973, no. 11.

twilight years in denmark

In 1972, Webster said of Copenhagen: "You've got some real jazz fans there. I got a lot of help from an eye doctor, doctor Godfresen. I came over from Amsterdam to tape something for the radio or TV in Copenhagen. I just said to him, 'I wouldn't mind having a house here.' He said, 'Are you looking for a place? I'll find you one.' And there you go—I've been living here for three years now."[1]

Webster's one-bedroom apartment was in the town center, on Nørre Søgade Street, alongside the river Peblinge Sø. Before he moved there, he stayed at hotels, and spent a few months staying with the Wolsgaard Iversen family. At Nørre Søgade 37, B4, he lived by himself; the front door was adorned with a sign that read "B.F. Webster." When he wasn't out on tour, he would often go for walks in the city parks, where he fed the ducks and swans.

He soon created a life for himself similar to his circumstances in Amsterdam. He built up a small circle of friends: Dr. Godfresen, pianist/arranger Billy Moore

(1917–1989), 27-year-old tenorist Jesper Thilo, record salesman Bent Kauling, nurse Birgit Nordtorp, singer Matty Peters, her husband Herman Wolsgaard Iversen, and their son, journalist and television producer Henrik Wolsgaard Iversen. He also stayed in contact with his friends in Amsterdam. In the summer of 1970, Steven Kwint and Egbert de Bloeme and his wife paid him a visit. The visitors stayed at a hotel and visited him often. Ben treated them to some hearty home-cooked beans and bacon.

His major support in the Danish capital was Birgit Nordtorp, a pleasant-looking blond woman in her early forties. She tried to save him from neglect in his twilight years. According to Ben's cousin Harley Robinson, her care was desperately needed. "If it hadn't been for Birgit, he probably would have died soon after he moved to Copenhagen." Although Nordtorp had her own apartment—in the town of Hundie, just outside Copenhagen—she was a regular visitor to his. Nordtorp remembers, "When I first saw him, I was really impressed. You could see he had a strong personality. He radiated great warmth, and he was intelligent. A snob he wasn't—he associated with young people and common people. If someone tried to act impressive, he looked right through it—it just didn't interest him.

"I think he needed me because I can't drink. I'm a perfectly normal person with a perfectly normal life. Whenever he had to go on tour, he needed someone to calm him down. And he liked knowing there was someone back home waiting for him."[2]

According to Rens Kwint, "Steven and Birgit were among the few people he trusted. They were very different friendships though. Birgit was a mother figure, the caring nurse type—a woman he sometimes spouted abuse at, but nonetheless deeply respected. Steven and Ben were buddies, good old boys together. Birgit's company did him a lot of good. She protected him from himself those last four years."

Ben got a lot of visitors. Billy Moore: "He was always listening to music. He would call me: 'Come over!' and I would come and he had his tape recorder or his record player going and he had a pipe into his bathroom too, so when he was taking a bath, or would go to sit on the throne, he didn't miss a beat."[3]

Tenor sax player Jesper Thilo: "He lived alone, and he really liked it when someone came by. I went over to his flat a lot. We'd have a beer or something stronger, and talk about music. He liked playing old Art Tatum tapes. Sometimes there was a plate of food getting moldy in a corner somewhere. Lord knows how long that had been standing there. I think he wanted the same role for himself that Coleman Hawkins had in New York. He wanted to help me with things he knew a lot about, like tone formation. He taught me a lot about embouchure, about how to develop a good sound."[4]

The summer of 1969 was quiet, although he did go on the odd small tour; in August, he played with trumpet player Rowland Greenberg in Norway. In the fall, he played with the Danish radio big band a few times—a group of highly trained musicians that included NHØP,

Thilo, and trumpeters Alan Botschinsky and Palle Mikkelborg.

In October, Wieringa made one more appearance in his life. That month, Webster recorded a record with Drew, NHØP, drummer Donald McKyre—an expatriate American—and Wieringa—which meant that there were two pianists. The reason is obvious: Wieringa made the saxophonist a lucrative offer so Webster thought, "Alright, you can play along, but I'll make sure to have a real pianist as well."

Wieringa's explanation for this odd ensemble is different (and doubtful): "Ben told me one time, 'I want to make a record where I'm surrounded by pianists.' He liked pianists a lot, you see. I said, 'Fine—which musicians do you have in mind?' He came up with this list. I took it to Bovema, and they agreed."

The resulting record, *Blow, Ben, Blow*, is only half an hour long—Bovema did not want to include a duet by the two pianists—and contains mostly simple tunes like "John Brown's Body" and "The Preacher."[5]

※

In Copenhagen, Webster's career didn't take off as much as he had hoped. Quite the contrary: his problems only increased. The quality of his concert performances varied greatly. He got heavier, had an increasingly difficult time walking, and drank more all the time. Ben Webster had become a depressive old man who could no longer summon the willpower to leave the bottle alone.

Billy Moore: "He'd work in one place for a while, then

somewhere else for a little. It was his own mistake. He'd accept gigs even when he was too drunk to play. Club owners didn't appreciate that. Sometimes Jesper Thilo had to take care of the solos, things like that. There were small scandals all the time. He would have had an easier time finding work if alcohol hadn't played such a dominating role in his life. That's why record companies were so reluctant. I went over to CBS one time and they said, 'We'd like to tape him, but...how's his health?' "[6]

In the first months of 1970, when the streets of Copenhagen were covered in ice, Ben broke his leg just above the ankle. It probably happened when he slipped getting out of a taxi. The fracture took a long time to heal, and the cane he often used already, now, for a time, became a necessity.

Writer Henk Romijn Meijer met him in Amsterdam on March 5. "I met him one more time, massive and a little down, at a Dizzy Gillespie concert in Frascati, with a hat on his head and a cane at his side, because he had broken his ankle [*sic*]. We talked a little and kept quiet about the promised meal [Romijn Meijer had promised to take him out for dinner some evening]... During the intermission, we said a kind of temporary goodbye. He died soon after."[7]

Alcohol made him mistrustful. Rens Kwint experienced this as well: "Whenever he was here, Steven always had to go along with him to get his money and look after his sax. He trusted almost no one anymore. Ben used to get a bit paranoid anyway whenever he was drinking. He had had bad experiences in the United States of course.

The whites who'd take advantage of the black guy. That notion never left him."

The result of this paranoia was a sudden end to his formerly close collaboration with Cees Slinger. The business that led to the break-up started out innocently enough. Albert Heijn, a large Dutch supermarket chain, asked Webster to make a record to showcase the tenorist's virtues—and the supermarket's, of course. Slinger was asked to take musical leadership of the enterprise. Slinger: "That record had to be made on an absolute shoestring budget. We were told to find pieces for which we'd need to pay no royalties because nobody was sure who wrote them, or because the composer had been dead for an awfully long time. Traditionals. The music publisher gave us a long list, and Ben and I made our choice. Because there were going to be four wind players we needed some arrangements, so I ended up writing those. I burned the midnight oil a few nights in a row, and that was that. Except for one, "Greensleeves." Herman Schoonderwalt had agreed to write that one."

On August 4, 1970, they practiced in the Amsterdam theater De Brakke Grond with the septet organized for the occasion. Singer Henny Vonk, who came over to listen, sang a few missing lines from two black spirituals. The next day, all the music was recorded in a provincial studio, and early in 1971 the record *Ben op Zijn Best* (*Ben at His Best*) appeared. The LP was available at Albert Heijn supermarkets for *f*4.95 ($2.50), and the small edition sold out within a few weeks.[8]

Cees Slinger: "We thought, well, that was that. But a

little while later, we were astonished to learn that the record had been reissued by RCA's French division. Neither Ben, I as the arranger, nor any of the other musicians had been informed about, let alone paid for this."

Irv Rochlin, an American pianist who had settled in the Netherlands, recalled that, "Six months after that recording, Ben and Steven were in Antwerp, and they needed to go to a supermarket. Ben saw a rack of records and Steven said, 'Why don't you stay here, I'll go and get the groceries.' And what happened? Ben found his Albert Heijn record between the albums. The same music, but with a different cover. He was furious."

Cees Slinger: "Ben was immediately convinced that I was behind all that. We had quite a long conversation about this, but I just couldn't convince him. He thought, 'That smooth talker Slinger must be behind this.' Look, he's black, I'm white and from an upper-middle-class background at that. I went to a prestigious school... All his old distrust came back in full force."

Both Cees and Ben obtained legal assistance. It transpired that trombone player George Kaatee and TV producer Hans Pohl had sold the tapes. Kaatee denied criminal intent. "Hans and I had organized that session. It was common practice that the producers paid the artists one lump sum, and then owned the tapes. We had just started out as producers, and were naive enough to think that that was the way things were going to work here. But the contract stated that Webster and Slinger were to make that record exclusively 'on behalf of Albert Heijn.' We simply overlooked those words.

"When that was pointed out to us, Hans Pohl, who had a law degree, immediately drew up a perfectly good contract with Ben Webster. Cees was very calm, but Webster and his lawyer got so overexcited about it that we decided to forgo our producers' royalties. We thought—it's a little jazz record, you won't get rich off that, it's not worth all this fuss. We never received one penny for that French edition. It was a learning experience for us."

Slinger: "I ran into Kaatee on the street one time and he said, 'Everything was done in haste, and we didn't know...' So we shook hands and decided to forget about it. I was much more upset about that break with Ben. That really distressed me. I actually felt worse for him than for myself. It was really tragic that the man had apparently had such terrible experiences that he could not even trust a good friend and colleague anymore. And we were such good friends before this incident. Afterward, he refused to play with me ever again.

"A few years later, he died. He was laid out in Amsterdam. I went over there, and there he lay. He looked very calm, as though he was sleeping. I stood there with a lump in my throat and I mumbled, 'Ben, man, I really had nothing to do with it.' Well, it was too late for that, of course."

Webster almost never discussed this incident with anybody; as far as he was concerned, anyone might overhear, and everything you said can and would be used against you. Drummer John Engels, who was

Slinger's partner for years and played on the Albert Heijn record as well, last saw him in Copenhagen, a few months before his death.

"I had a gig there with Louis van Dijk and Jacques Schols. I was sitting in the hotel, had a drink, and guess who walked in? Ben Webster. It was kind of a pathetic affair, because he was falling-down drunk. But he did recognize me and was overjoyed to see me. He started hugging me, and kept shouting, 'My man!' And then he started to cry. I didn't know where to look. He was very moved. He wanted to know everything, what I was working on and how I was doing."

Engels didn't know about the Albert Heijn matter either. But when I told him about it, he said that that might explain Ben's behavior.

⨳

Toward the end of 1970, the Danes were gradually getting used to Ben's drinking problem. There was virtually no hope for recovery. Jesper Thilo said, "There were no day and night for him. When he was asleep he slept very soundly, and when he was awake, he was wide-awake. He didn't follow society's rules, and consequently ended up in situations where he needed help.

"There were times when he was asleep when we came to pick him up, so we would make sure to be a few hours early. And if we were really unlucky, he'd fall asleep on stage. It would apparently be night for him. Very strange. But right up to the end there were nights when he was completely lucid and played like he did when he was 35."[9]

In October, a reasonably smooth concert took place at Ronnie Scott's. He also recorded an album with strings that month in England.[10] On the day of his return to Copenhagen, he was expected back at a rehearsal with the Danish big band. After he had kept the orchestra waiting for several hours, his friend Herman Wolsgaard Iversen (singer and presenter Matty Peters' husband) was sent to fetch him.

After repeated knocking and ringing, a sleepy, craggy voice yelled, "Who? Who th' hell is there?" Forty minutes later, washed, shaven, and dressed, he entered the recording studio. This afternoon was taped without his knowledge, and to his great dismay: he had used language that Mayme and Mom wouldn't have approved. The rehearsal appeared posthumously as *No Fool, No Fun.*[11]

The A side contains rehearsals for his own "composition" "Did You Call Her Today," a riff over the chords of "In A Mellow Tone." The guest soloist was not happy with the phrasing, and issued all kinds of wild instructions. At one point he asked the orchestra to play a certain phrase "like 'I'm tired, motherfucker!' " Or he'd shout "Bam! Bam!" and "Hit them notes!"

The musicians started talking and laughing a little among themselves in Danish, and Webster thought they were making fun of him. Matty Peters and her husband also kept a close eye on his beer consumption—another thing he wasn't too happy about. In the ballad "Old Folks," he thought the intro was "too pretty." "I should make a pirouette after this," he said. He dragged himself up out of his chair and, with an annoyed look on his face, made a turn balancing on one leg, like a genuine ballerina. The orchestra members fell over each other laughing.

※

The year 1971 yielded not a single record, discounting two pieces that appeared on compilation albums twenty years later.[12] Only in 1933 and 1950 had his discography been so meager. He did, however, keep concertizing.

Henrik Wolsgaard Iversen: "Ben had the impractical habit of keeping two pocket calendars in which he alternatively wrote his bookings up. Sometimes this resulted in double bookings—or close. Thus, a festival in Italy and a gig in Finland could be placed within a few hours interval and since he would only travel by train, he could manage to be several days late for gigs."[13]

By coincidence he got a jazz musician as a neighbor in 1971: Keith Smith, a British trumpet player who became part of Papa Bue's Viking Jazz Band, a Danish "trad" orchestra. Both this orchestra and a combo with Ben Webster were part of a performance in a huge concert hall in Oslo. It was one of the few large concerts for which anyone had dared ask the old tenorist. The crown prince of Norway was in the audience. After the concert, the prince sent down a footman to inform the orchestra leaders he would like to meet them up in his box.

Smith remembered: "Ben was having a 'taste' in one corner but assured the departing company that he'd soon catch them up. At this point, it's worth mentioning that Ben was greatly overweight, but his legs were really thin—rather like inadequate stilts. The other band leaders were through with their formal introductions and the bowing and walking backwards bit when the distinct sound of curses and groans grew uncomfortably nearer, echoing up the grand staircase with great audibility. Ben, having finally completed his ascent, staggered through the door breathing copiously and swaying past the neat pleats of the velvet curtains made his entrance. The aide—almost speechless at the break in decorum—proceeded with his introductions, 'Your Royal Highness, this is Ben Webster.' The Crown Prince nodded regally, and the aide continued, 'Mr. Webster, may I present his Royal Highness The Crown Prince of Norway,' pointing Ben nervously in the right direction, at which point Ben lunged forward, slapped the Crown Prince on the back, yelling 'Ben Webster, King of the Tenors—pleased to meet you, Prince!' "[14]

However droll such episodes were, Webster's state was really cause for alarm. Joe Zawinul visited Europe in 1971, with his new jazz-rock outfit Weather Report. He later recalled that Webster was stone drunk and almost fell on top of his electric piano. He congratulated Zawinul for getting "famous," but complained that this new music was "too loud."[15]

Birgit Nordtorp: "It's not easy to be friends with someone who drinks a lot... Whenever he came home drunk and went to bed, I'd just let him sleep and hoped he'd feel better in the morning. But that wasn't always the case. There were times when he'd go drinking for many days in a row. Sometimes I could stand it, but not always."[16] In the fall of 1971, her relationship with Ben was at an all-time low. She didn't visit for a few months, and a number of other friends refused to see him as well.

Fortunately, he was occasionally still able to play. In May 1971 he toured Holland, without Slinger of course, but with Spanish pianist Tete Montoliu and Dutchmen Henk Haverhoek (bass) and Eric Ineke (drums). Before this, in April, he had been to London for a two-week gig—shorter than usual—at Ronnie Scott's, with pianist Stan Tracey, bassist Dave Green, and drummer Tony Crombie.

Journalist Benny Green attended the London date for *The Observer*, and noted that the sax player, suffering from shortness of breath, just played solos in phrases of two to four measures. He only played sitting down, took long breaks between pieces, and was not about to tire himself out with any up tempos. But his tone was still intact, and that made up for a lot in Green's opinion. "He is a musician whose tone is so distinctive that it would be an entertainment, even to eavesdrop on his scale practice."[17]

November 7, 1971 was a momentous day—the day Duke Ellington came to Copenhagen. Nordtorp: "Ben loved it when Ellington's orchestra was visiting. He'd try to stay sober on those occasions."[18] The orchestra played in the Tivoli Gardens that afternoon and evening, and at the leader's request, his former sideman played along on some pieces. Ellington made an attempt to reconstruct the old "Cotton Tail," which failed utterly: Webster was no longer capable of such a musical tour de force.

Ellington tenorist Harold Ashby: "During the break [between the two shows] we went over to Ben's house. He cooked a bean dish with rice. There was a lot to drink... We were all sitting around talking. Ben even played some piano for us, stride piano. He had a clarinet he showed [saxophonist] Russell Procope."[19]

Copenhagen acquaintance Bent Kauling recalled: "Mercer [Ellington] had called him a couple of days before. Ben was so excited. The band came to town around two-thirty, but Ben—at ten o'clock he was ready! He had his hair dyed, his shoes were shining, he was sitting there like a kid going to his first prom or something! He was 63, and acting like a little boy."[20]

※

From late 1971 onward, Ben regularly played in the Netherlands again. His pianists were the American Irv Rochlin (who had moved to Amsterdam that year), Spaniard Tete Montoliu, and (on ten occasions) Dutchman Rob Agerbeek. The bass was usually played by Rob Langereis or Henk Haverhoek, and percussion by Eric Ineke, Peter Ypma, or (preferably) Tony Inzalaco, an American who had moved to Cologne and did a lot of studio work there. Inzalaco stayed in Europe from 1968 through 1978, after which he moved to Boston.

Webster's Dutch performances were mostly limited to small auditoriums and clubs. Paradiso had lost its reputation as a jazz center after Hans Dulfer stopped organizing programs, and its successor, the Bimhuis, didn't open until a year after Ben's death, on October 1, 1974.

Ben Webster's final studio dates were on June 5 and November 28, 1972. At these sessions, he recorded LPs in Paris, then Spain—neither of which was particularly good.[21] He also had a guest soloist spot with the group Savage Rose. Only one song with this Danish formation was ever issued. Record studios were apprehensive about asking him—they knew about his 'personal problems,' and studio hours are expensive. The young Danish label Steeplechase found a solution: producer Nils Winther and Ben agreed to record a number of concerts in Montmartre, in January and April, 1973. That was a less risky undertaking for the label. The recordings resulted in *My Man*, the last decent album of Webster's career.[22]

※

It appears there was a small Ben revival in the first half of 1973. It may have been that he himself realized the end of his career was nigh, and resolved to show the world one more time what he was capable of. He did so in the Netherlands in February, May, and September, 1973.

On May 31, he performed as a guest soloist with the Dutch Swing College Band and the Metropole Orkest, which organized a lavish promenade concert in the southern city of Breda. According to a newspaper reporter, his condition was so poor that his performance with the Metropole Orkest was cut off after just two numbers: a couple of broad-shouldered gentlemen stepped onto the stage, pulled the sax out of his mouth, and pressed a huge bouquet of flowers into his hand.[23]

One of the accompanying musicians in Breda, guitarist Arie Ligthart, remembered that Ben was lit. "He could hardly stand on his own two legs. He let the bottle go around the dressing room—that was the kind of guy he was. He was an amiable fellow. I remember he played "Mood Indigo" and "That's All." Ben played very few notes. But strangely enough, they were all notes that had to be there, and all right on target. I thought that was nothing short of a miracle, considering the shape he was in."

In the summer of 1973, he went on an 11-night tour of Denmark with Harry Edison and Benny Carter. Webster got very sentimental about seeing Carter again, and sometimes, when a ballad was going well, tears ran down his cheeks. This happened more than once during his final year, and made his Danish friends quite uncomfortable. The old tenorist simply told Jesper Thilo, "I cry because I play so beautiful."[24]

Pianist Jimmy Rowles, his old friend "Shithouse" from L.A., was the last old friend he met. In July of 1973, Rowles traveled to Europe with Carmen McRae. When he had a week off he went to Copenhagen, where he slept on Ben's couch.

Rowles: "He wasn't in good shape. He was drinking a lot and his legs hurt him, and he was enormous. He never wore anything the whole time but his shorts, and he'd sit in a little swivel chair and talk about 'the Judge,' which is what he called Milt Hinton. Ben was a Jekyll-

and-Hyde. He was a sensitive cat, and when he wasn't drinking he was soft-spoken and polite and as gentle as cream. But after two drinks, forget it. Benny Carter was the only man he'd listen to when he was like that. If Ben was roaring around and Carter happened to be there, he'd say, 'Cut it out, Ben. Go sit down and behave yourself,' and Ben would. Ben used to say of Carter, 'There's a man who can bake a cake as light as a feather and whip any man.' One night in Copenhagen, we put Ben to bed—there were always people flowing in and out—and went out to see the sights. I got back late, and there was Ben stretched out on the marble floor like a gingerbread man. I still don't know how I got him into bed again. When I had to leave to meet Carmen, Ben hung out the window, still in his shorts, his huge shoulders and chest bare, and waved and waved and kept saying, 'Come back, S.H.,' which is what we called each other. 'Come back and see me soon.' A few weeks later, the cable came saying that he had passed away."[25]

notes

1 *Jazz Hot*, September 1972.

2 From the movie *The Brute and the Beautiful* by John Jeremy (1989).

3 See note 2.

4 See note 2.

5 The songs on this album have been included on the CD version of *For the Guv'nor*, Affinity.

6 See note 2.

7 Henk Romijn Meijer, *Een Blauwe Golf aan de Kust* (Meulenhoff 1986).

8 *I Remember*, RCA 741060/Black Elephant 822005 (LP).

9 See note 2.

10 *Ben Webster's Dictionary*, Philips 6308101 (LP).
11 *No Fool, No Fun*, Spotlite.
12 *Plays Ballads*, Storyville, and *Plays Duke Ellington*, Storyville.
13 Cover text to the album *No Fool, No Fun* (See note 11.)
14 Cover text to the album *Ben Webster in Europe*, Rarities 45 (LP).
15 Cover text to the album *Trav'lin Light*, Milestone M-47056.
16 See note 2.
17 *The Observer*, April 25, 1971.
18 See note 2.
19 See note 2.
20 See note 2.
21 *Autumn Leaves*, Futura Swing, and *Gentle Ben*, Ensayo.
22 *My Man*, Steeplechase (CD).
23 *Utrechts Nieuwblad*, June 1, 1973.
24 See note 2.
25 Whitney Balliet: *Barney, Bradley and Max* (Oxford University Press 1989).

the final tours

Pianist Irv Rochlin: "It was late '71, and I had been living on the outskirts of Amsterdam for a few months when I got a phone call from Steven Kwint. He told me that Ben Webster was in the city. Ben was staying at hotel De Haas in the Vondelstraat. That hotel was full of jazz musicians visiting the Netherlands. Dexter Gordon always stayed there as well. Steven asked me if I wanted to come over to his house to talk to Ben. Ben needed a pianist. They had already found a bass player and a drummer: Henk Haverhoek and Tony Inzalaco.

"We sat around talking for a while, and after fifteen minutes Steven asked:
'Do you have a car?'
'Yeah, do you want to go somewhere?'
"Ben said, 'Let's just go for a drive, it doesn't matter where.'
"We drove around Amsterdam some, and I dropped them off on the way back. I thought it was all kind of weird. The next day, Steven called to tell me that everything was OK, and that I was going on tour with Ben Webster. I said, 'What was that all about, yesterday?

Why did we go for that drive?'

"Steven replied, 'Ben wanted to see if you are a good driver. You will always have to drive him because you are the only one who also lives in Amsterdam.' I asked him if we didn't need to do an audition. 'That was the audition,' Steven said. That's how I got that job with Ben. But I'd also been recommended by Dexter Gordon, who was also living in Copenhagen at the time. Apparently that was enough.

"I worked with him until he died, almost two years later. During that time, we went on five or six tours that lasted two or three weeks each. So I've done about fifty concerts with Ben in total. All those concerts were organized by impresario Wim Wigt. He was really young and inexperienced at the time. Things went wrong sometimes, and Ben couldn't handle that very well.

"One day, we played in Germany, in Düsseldorf. It was a small basement: the bar was upstairs and the auditorium downstairs, just like the Subway in Cologne. It was the last day of the tour, and Ben had asked Wim to reserve a seat in a sleeping car, allowing him to return to Copenhagen the same night. But Wim hadn't done it. Wim had called the club owner and asked him to arrange that train for Ben, but the guy had forgotten.

"I came in with Ben, and we saw that Wim was there. Ben started talking to Wim, and I went ahead downstairs. After a while Ben came trudging down the stairs and started drinking hard, right from the first set. I thought, 'The man is upset about something.' He never drank without reason—there was always a cause.

"After the gig we went upstairs, where we found Wim again. Ben walked up to Wim and said, 'You're a young cat, and you may learn. But I doubt it.' The next morning, I drove him to Central Station.

"There were more annoying instances like that. We were in a beautiful little theater one time that had an ancient piano with a beautiful tone, and Ben was very content at the start of the first set. He had brought some folders with parts for his accompanists. They had been written by British pianist Stan Tracey, and almost all the chords were fine.

"At one point, Ben turned around and called "Sophisticated Lady." That's a well-known piece, but Rob [Langereis] and I went ahead and opened the folders anyway, in case there were any changes in there. When we got to the end of the second A, at the transition to the bridge, we saw a number of strange chords. Robbie and I looked at each other and decided to go ahead and play them. We thought, 'Maybe Ben wants to do something special over there.'

"We played exactly what it said, but it sounded very odd. Then we modulated to the bridge, which was in G as usual, but Ben had ended up in C. We just stayed in G, to prevent even greater chaos. Well, that moment of confusion ruined the whole night. Ben didn't say a word, but started drinking during the break after the first set. The second set was bad.

"When that set was over and the audience had left, Ben came up to me. 'What happened on "Sophisticated Lady"?' he snarled at me. When Ben was in a mood like that, it was no use arguing with him. He wouldn't listen to what you had to say anyway. He sat down at the piano and played "Sophisticated Lady." But when he got to the bridge, he modulated to C again! In a piece he had been playing for decades! I said to him, 'Ben, that's exactly what you did when we were playing!' He immediately jumped up from the piano and said 'What!' After that, there was no more reasoning with him. I never understood how things turned out that way.

"The best concert took place in Alphen aan de Rijn. That was in '72, with Tony and Henk. There was an enormous hall with a very low stage, not much more than a foot off the floor. The outside wall was directly behind the stage—there were no dressing rooms. We played two sets and it was perfect. I felt so good after that concert... And yet something strange happened again.

"At the end of the second set we got a thundering ovation, and the audience wanted an encore. Ben played just one more piece, but then he considered his job done. He went over to the side of the stage and started putting his sax away while people were shouting, 'More, More!' Ben put his hat on his head, shot the people an incensed look, and shouted as loud as possible, 'MORE WHAT??!!' By which he meant, 'What the hell are you thinking, I've worked my butt off, won't you allow me my well-earned rest?'

"In his final years, he walked with a cane. I always asked him, 'How do you feel. Ben?' 'Are you alright, Ben?' He got so tired of all those questions that he growled 'I'm just fine!' one night, real loud. When I picked him up at the station for the next concert, he no longer carried the cane.

"I can't say what percentage of concerts went wrong. The first set was often good, the second mediocre, and the third—if we played a third at all—bad. On the whole, he was easy to play with. He always kept time and stayed within the right chords. Even when he was out of practice he never made basic mistakes. We never had so save him, like we did with Dexter Gordon. The only problems were that he played few choruses and that his phrases were short; he didn't finish them as nicely as he used to."

Rochlin remembered that Webster could no longer remember the names of Dutch musicians. "After a solo he'd gesture to the soloist in question and shout, 'Mr. Pianoman!', 'Mr. Bassman!', or 'Mr. Drummerman!'—and that was that."

Pianist Rob Agerbeek: "He'd always yell 'Pianoman!' or 'Bassman!' and then you had to get up and politely receive the applause. If you didn't stand up, he ordered you to 'Come on! Stand up and bow!' I'd think to myself, what's this circus all about? But Ben took it very seriously. That was the way things ought to be done.

"I did about twelve concerts with Ben, through 1972 and 1973. As a replacement for Irv. Ben appeared to be quite happy with me. He always yelled, 'My man!' or 'Hey, pianoman!' when he first saw me. Then he'd give me a hug, and just about squash me. That guy was strong as an ox. He was a giant.

"I did have a hard time with the fact that he made me play pieces I barely knew, and in the original key at that. And Ben was not the person to want to discuss that. He never said, 'What do you think we should play next?' No, he called out a title, counted down, and then you were supposed to start playing right away. One time, he said, "Stardust." 'Oh, fine, in C I assume?' I replied. 'Oh no!' Ben replied, 'in D flat.' A very difficult key on the piano, but that happened to be what the piece was originally in. And when I hesitated for a moment, he gestured at me impatiently and said, 'Make an intro, pianoman, an intro!'

"Fortunately, I was familiar with most of his repertoire: "How High the Moon," "In a Mellow Tone"... He threw me in at the deep end and it wasn't easy, but it was the only way he'd work. I wouldn't have dreamed of saying, 'Ben, why don't we play that in a different key?' That would have been really embarrassing. He just assumed we were up to anything.

"It was a bad idea to ask him too many questions on stage, because his mood could turn at any moment. To him, everything was obvious: this is how a certain piece is played, and there's nothing to ask about it. If you did, he'd sulk, 'Stop complaining, I've been playing it like this for more than forty years.' His grumbling would turn into mumbles under his breath, three quarters of which you couldn't even make out.

"I did a concert with both Dexter and Ben once. That's when I learned how little it took to upset him. At some point it was time to play a ballad, and Ben suggested

"Body and Soul." I played an introduction, after which Ben joined with a few deep sighs, like only he could.

"While Ben was blowing his solo, Dexter leaned over to me and said, 'When it's my turn, let's go Coltrane style.' You know, with slightly different chords and a chromatic bass line. I didn't see why not. So after Ben had told his story, Dexter tapped me on the shoulder and I switched to Coltrane chords. At which Ben just went into this tirade of, 'Hey, what kind of nonsense is this!'

"But I kept playing, because we were on stage after all. Dexter began to play, and meanwhile Ben was yelling abuse, 'Hey motherfucker, how dare you, this is not how you play this piece, who do you think you are, you upstart, come on, listen to me...' And he just wouldn't stop. Dexter acted like he didn't hear anything. I've got that whole fight on tape. Dexter even tried to talk to him, along the lines of, 'Just let us do our thing, the local cats like to play it this way sometimes as well.' But Ben was livid. He played one or two more pieces, and then left Dexter to finish the show.

"Afterward, we all had to drive home in the same car together, to hotel De Haas in Amsterdam. Ben sat in the front with Wim Wigt, Dexter in the back with Ria Wigt. Dexter was very calm, but Ben just kept whining. And after he had given him a piece of his mind, he even went on to say that Dexter had better not try anything with the lady—something Dexter would never have dreamed of doing—or he would be in trouble with Ben. The next day, Ben and Dexter were put on a plane to Copenhagen, and the fight continued. It lasted for about a month and a half.

"Dexter later told me, 'I was playing at Montmartre with a Danish group and guess who walked in? Ben Webster. With a gold lighter. Ben walked up to me during the break and said, "This is for you. Let's forget it." '

"The quality of his playing varied considerably. At the first three concerts, he was great. He was going all-out and I thought, I know you're a bit older than on those *Jazz at the Philharmonic* records, but you've still got the same approach, the same dedication, the same ideas, and a good embouchure. But in the short time I knew the man, it got harder and harder for him. As though he was sick.

"In between pieces it would be quiet for a few moments, and you could hear him mumbling, 'Now what shall we play next?' He'd be looking around a little confused, and after a while he'd say, 'Oh yeah, Mr. pianoman, let's play...' As though he'd blacked out for a while. And he'd complain after a solo, grumble about malfunctioning keys, turn around real slowly to find his glass... He was really having a difficult time.

"His play got erratic. He only played brief, foreshortened lines. His solos lasted for two or three choruses, and then he let us take at least ten. If I wanted to stop, he called, 'Yeah, pianoman, one more! Okay, one more!' That was distressing. Because you build up a solo after all, then work toward the end, and right at the moment where he was supposed to take over, you had to start all over again.

"The minimal solo he then produced was all Ben when

it came to tone formation, though. That tone stayed intact. But it cost him a tremendous effort. He sweated copiously... always had a handkerchief out.

"He also started giving short speeches to win time—something he never used to do. He'd say, 'The piece I'm gonna play now I've played many times before with my old buddy Duke Ellington, the great Duke Ellington you all know, and my pianist said, "Why don't you play that one again some time," so I thought, 'Let's dust this one off and see if I can still do it.' "

Drummer Pierre Courbois: "In 1971 I played with Ben for a while. Not that often—I think we may have spent about a week touring together. Ben was in good shape; if I played with brushes too much, he'd yell, 'Sticks!' He didn't want any careful treatment.

"The week before, my four-year-old son Barend—who now plays bass guitar with Jasper van 't Hof—had been run over by a moped. He had suffered a serious brain injury. So during the daytime, I was in the hospital at his bedside. At night I told Ben about this, and later he'd always ask me about how 'Barney' was doing. He really cared. On the last evening, he came over and gave me a Lego car, 'For Barney,' he said. I'll never forget that."

Drummer Eric Ineke: "Tony Inzalaco was usually his drummer. But Tony did a lot of studio work. He lived in Cologne, and regularly had to play with people like Kurt Edelhagen. When he couldn't make it, they called me to stand in. I think I did about ten concerts with him in '71, '72 and '73.

"The first time I was nervous as hell. I was only 24, and

there were so many wild stories going around, about knife fights and such. I thought, 'Jesus, I hope I survive!' I went to that first gig with fear and trepidation. That was in '71, I believe we played in Wilhelmina [The Netherlands]. When I got there, I saw a hugely fat man in a leather jacket and a leather hat. He slowly got up, breathing heavily, and gave me a big welcome, 'Nice to meet you!' My fears had been unfounded.

"How did you play drums behind Ben Webster? You kept it simple, straightforward, with a light Jo Jones-style afterbeat. He didn't like you to get in his way with fancy work. When it was going well, he'd turn around and say encouragingly, 'My man!'

"You did have to get used to the fact that he mostly played laid back. As the drummer, you still had to keep the tempo tight, of course. I was lucky that I mostly played with Rob Langereis. We were in Rob Agerbeek's quintet together, so we knew each other through and through. But I can imagine that a less experienced accompanist might have let the tempo slow down. You really had to watch that.

"With Dexter, that was even more problematic. He would sometimes fall several measures behind. You really had to be right on top of the beat—extremely hard work. After my first tour with Dexter I looked like the living dead. It was much easier with Ben. I always came home relaxed, feeling I'd had a good time that night.

"In those days, Dutch groups usually had to play three sets. But Ben usually wanted to play only two, which I liked. That kind of guy could make demands, of course.

When everyone got tired, he'd say, 'I'm playing two sets and no more,' and everyone would be nodding agreement. He kept his authority right up to the end."

records in the decade 1964–1973

In the sixties, Webster was rarely in for challenges, or open to new influences. He played his well-known licks in up tempo, and in medium to slow tempos his solos mainly stayed within established contours. Once he had found an "ideal" solo, he usually saw no need to make revisions.

This is well illustrated by a comparison between "My Romance" played with Michael Renzi in the summer of 1964,[1] with Kenny Drew on January 30, 1965,[2] with Arnved Meyer on September 15, 1965,[3] and with Irv Rochlin on September 6, 1973.[4] Or "You'd Be So Nice To Come Home To" recorded with Hawkins on October 16, 1957,[5] with the Alex Welsh rhythm section on April 4, 1967,[6] and with Slinger on April 8, 1968.[7] Or "Danny Boy" with Peterson on May 21, 1953,[8] and with Drew on January 30, 1965.[9]

There's not much variation in his other standard repertory pieces either, including "That's All," "Lover Come Back to Me," "Sunday," "Our Love Is Here to Stay," "In a Mellow Tone," "Autumn Leaves," and "Old Folks." You can hardly hold this uniformity against him. How much innovation can you expect of a man who has been in the business thirty or forty years, and all that time worked hard on developing a highly personal style? It was more important that, given the right circumstances, the "Dutch master" could still play music with authority and conviction.

Unfortunately, only two official albums were recorded during his residence in Amsterdam, one of which was recorded with inferior accompaniment, and the other with mediocre sound quality. I'm talking about *At Ease* with Frans Wieringa's amateur trio, and *For the Guv'nor* with Slinger–Schols–Engels.[10] The fact that the second session had to be pushed forward when Ben suddenly moved to Copenhagen is indicative of the dearth of opportunities. It also helps explain why his stay in the Netherlands is ignored by most jazz books—including the otherwise dependable *New Grove Dictionary of Jazz*.[11] Too bad the Dutch jazz scene didn't learn much from this negligence. Other mainstream tenorists—Don Byas (1912–1972), Sandy Mosse (1929–1983), and Ruud Brink (1937–1990), to name but a few—didn't seem to exist either.

In other European countries the record industry's interest was greater, but not overwhelming either. If Webster had mainly come to Europe for studio work, he might as well have stayed home. In 1960–1964, his final lean years in the U.S., he made an average of one LP per year as leader or co-leader, and three more as a sideman; in Europe, he recorded approximately one-and-a-half records as (co-)leader per year, and he was invited for hardly any guest solo recordings. One mitigating circumstance that should be mentioned is that Webster's European years happened to coincide with a period when interest in jazz was at an all-time low throughout the world, mainly due to the rise of pop. Webster moved to Europe right after the Beatles' first successes—their sensational first and only visit to Holland had taken place on June 5–7, 1964. Ben passed away right before the jazz revival of the mid-seventies.

Jopie Byas, Don's widow, remembered that there was little work for jazz musicians in those days. "My husband didn't record a single album in the Netherlands, as far as I know. And that while he lived in Amsterdam for seventeen years. Look, everything that came from the States got people's attention. But my husband had been here for such a long time that the novelty had worn off. Everyone said, 'Don Byas is living here, so we don't have to hurry asking him for a record date.' They just kept saying that until he got sick and died, and then it was too late.

"Before we went to Amsterdam, we lived in France. He usually worked in nightclubs there. We witnessed the first discotheques opening up in France. Jazz went out of style, and club owners learned that you could also fill your club simply playing records. That's what did jazz in."

Because Byas recorded almost no albums in Europe—exceptions were an EP with Rob Madna and others in 1962, and the record with Webster—Jopie received no royalties to speak of after her husband's death in 1972. "When my husband died our youngest child was three, and the eldest was ten. So I mostly raised them by myself. We had a hard time making ends meet. The children were musically gifted, but I could not afford any music lessons. I counted myself lucky when I had enough to feed and clothe them properly."

※

In spite of the difficult circumstances, Ben's stay in Denmark started out full of promise. On January 30 and 31, 1965, the label Black Lion recorded two of his concerts in the Copenhagen club Montmartre. The tapes provided enough music for three entire LPs. The music is consistently on such a high level that it is hard to pick out any highlights. Webster is in good shape, the accompanying artists understand him implicitly, and the recording quality leaves little to be desired.

Drummer Alex Riel gives you plenty of opportunity to regret that he hasn't done more on the international scene since. NHØP still really had to tug on the strings—bass amplifiers practically didn't exist—which enhanced his tone.[12]

The trio and the tenorist were possibly in even better form when they played a radio concert on March 4, 1965, later available as a bootleg. The musicians had grown used to each other by then, and attack all the standards with vigor.[13]

In September 1965, Black Lion had Webster come to a Copenhagen studio three times: once with the aforementioned trio, and twice with trumpeter Arnved Meyer's sextet. The results of these sessions, too, are satisfactory. The sextet tried for the style of a mid-sized

Ellington formation—a worthy effort. Tenorist Ole Kongsted so closely resembles Webster on "Brother John's Blues" that cover text writer Albert McCarthy fell for it, and thought he was hearing two Webster solos. Kongsted actually takes the first solo.[14]

After this grand prelude things got quiet—real quiet. His next session as a leader wasn't until almost a year and a half later. However, some concerts were transferred to records posthumously. One of these is a performance in Paris with Earl Hines. Webster plays an outstanding, sober version of "Sweet Lorraine," and almost blows Don Byas off the stage with his dazzling solo in "St. Louis Blues."[15]

On March 19, 1966, he was a guest at the small orchestra of Steen Vig, a Danish tenorist who had paid close attention to the young Coleman Hawkins. Unfortunately, Vig's rhythm section gave a compelling demonstration of how not to swing, which hardly enabled Webster to play even his most routine phrases.[16] Naturally, he was in better company when he appeared as a guest on three pieces with Duke Ellington in Juan-les-Pins.[17]

It took until January 11, 1967, before Webster finally entered a recording studio again, but that session fortunately resulted in one of the best records of his European years. British musicians Spike Heatley (bass) and Tony Crombie (drums) and American Dick Katz (piano) play delightfully, and the recording quality is superb. Although Webster stays on familiar territory, the session is almost up there with the two highly regarded recordings with Oscar Peterson on which he is the only wind player. Unfortunately, Katz is suffering from an over-active left hand—he doesn't seem to realize there is a bass player present. This session was later reissued, along with three pieces where Webster is accompanied by deadly boring pianist Allen Haven.[18]

Two records dating from April 1967—one with tenor players Eddie Miller, Eddie "Lockjaw" Davis, and Bud Freeman, and one with trumpeter Bill Coleman—are mutilated by the rhythm section of the Alex Welsh Band. Their rigid adherence to the beat is especially disastrous in ballads.[19]

The tenor record illustrates what happens when you combine mediocre accompaniment with a few hastily improvised themes: a painful regurgitation of old clichés. On top of that, Webster had an additional reason to hold back. According to writer Henk Romijn Meijer, he wanted to protect Freeman. " 'I've always loved Bud,' Ben said after a tour of England that also included Bud Freeman, 'and you can't do that to people like him.' By which he meant that you can't blow people like him out of the water."[20]

To get to the next official record sessions, we have to make a leap of nearly a year. But, again, the results are disappointing. This is the German record with Byas, which has been covered earlier.[21] Webster grumbled to Romijn Meijer that "He's trying to beat me with his quick notes." On April 8, 1968, the "Dutch Masters" made a more successful recording in Hilversum, the Netherlands. Two of the pieces recorded that day were included on a bootleg LP.[22]

About *At Ease* (January 12, 1969), the infamous LP with country amateurs, enough has been said already. However, it's worth noting once more the drummer's stupefying lack of imagination; the bassist who could play only one riff in the blues scale (and out of tune at that); and the clunky Peterson imitations by Wieringa.[23]

Just shy of two weeks later, Webster played in Lurelei, where de Bloeme was continuing the Jazzart series. The concert, taped by Egbert de Bloeme with simple equipment, was transferred to vinyl in 1989. A record full of beautiful tenor solos and with a solid background, but very poor balance; it is like a curse afflicted the Dutch recordings. De Bloeme: "I only had two microphones. I placed one over by Ben, and the other I slid into the bridge of the bass. I thought the percussion would be audible anyway. I was wrong. And Cees Slinger got the worst deal of all."

On March 10, 1969, Ben played with Jay McShann and alto saxophonist Eddie "Cleanhead" Vinson in a café in Antwerp, Belgium. Part of that session later appeared on a typical bootleg LP: bad sound quality, and it has, in any case, been nearly impossible to get your hands on a copy for years. The music, reminiscent of Kansas City in the thirties, is quite enjoyable.[24]

On May 26, 1969, shortly before Webster left for Copenhagen, *For the Guv'nor* was recorded.[25] And again, something went wrong with the balance. Dubiez explained: "The track that contained Ben malfunctioned. The technicians later tried to balance the sax with the other instruments, but they never managed to get it quite right."

A second handicap was the fact that Webster didn't feel the need to put his heart and soul into the recording. He may have been a bit apprehensive about saying goodbye to Holland and starting a new life elsewhere.

Drummer John Engels: "At the beginning of the session, he said, 'Let's just record everything in one go.' I believe it took us only three hours to record an entire LP." Cees Slinger's accompaniment is remarkably good, with a suitable, relatively modern approach. About a week after this hasty session, Ben Webster was back in Copenhagen.

※

Four records from his final years stand out: a concert that was released two decades later, titled *Live in Paris*; the Albert Heijn record; *My Man*, a compilation of Danish live recordings; and finally *Gentle Ben*, the session in Barcelona with Tete Montoliu. The compilations entitled *Ballads, Plays Duke Ellington* and *Master of Jazz* are of lesser quality, but do contain worthwhile moments. The Albert Heijn record is the best. The grocery chain's penny-pinching—the musicians were restricted to a copyright-free zone—forced Webster to deviate from his iron-clad repertory. The climax is "Nobody Knows...", a spiritual that Webster takes command of, as he does the traditionals "Ida Sweet as Apple Cider" and "Deep River." Readers of this book don't need to be told that *Steff's Shoes* is dedicated to Steven Kwint.[26]

Gentle Ben, recorded in Barcelona less than a year before Webster's death, also contains an ode to a good friend,

"My Nephew Bent"—Bent Kauling. The recording quality is excellent, presenting Ben's sensual sound to full advantage. His deteriorating health is showing, though; especially in "How Long Has This Been Going On" you can often hear the old horn player gasping for breath.[27]

My Man contains a few pieces above mid-tempo: "Sunday" and "I Got Rhythm." Webster plays short solos here that sound rather perfunctory. Although he does better in the ballads, you can tell that his decline, already evident on *Gentle Ben*, has advanced even further. The accompanists do a good job, but sound a little tinny on the record.[28]

The sound quality on *Live in Paris*, on the other hand, is extraordinary. This record is a registration of the November 4, 1972 concert with Georges Arvanitas' trio.[29]

Ben Webster's Dictionary, recorded with a large orchestra in London in 1970, was a missed opportunity. Ben really did his best, but the violin sauce the producer poured over his solos makes the music nearly impossible to digest.[30]

Due to poor recording quality and a tired-sounding soloist, the studio session on June 5, 1972—again with Arvanitas' trio—is not what one might have hoped. Drummer Charles Saudrais' countless frenzied figures were put on tape too prominently, which does little to enhance the swing.[31]

In May 1972, two Dutch concerts with Tete Montoliu were recorded that were later issued on vinyl. In both cases, the percussionist sounds far from light—Tony Inzalaco is downright lumbering at times, and Eric

Ineke still had a lot to learn as well. Webster played his familiar ballads once more, performed his usual choruses in the other two pieces, and left his accompanists to do most of the work.[32]

His new adventures with Frans Wieringa (*Blow Ben, Blow*) and the rehearsal with the Danish radio orchestra (*No Fool, No Fun*) were discussed earlier in this book. I'd like to add that *Blow Ben, Blow* is only interesting for those looking to complete their collection, and that *No Fool, No Fun* is worth buying mainly for Ben's conversations with the studio musicians.[33]

The bootleg label Rarities brought out recordings with "unknown Scandinavian musicians." These include—on "Perdido" and "Stardust"—enjoyable swing quartets with Norwegian trumpeter Rowland Greenberg, apparently a Roy Eldridge disciple. The record also contains "That's All," played by the Dutch Metropole Orkest. Here, four months before his death, Webster doesn't venture beyond his characteristic melodies.[34]

A number of Scandinavian live recordings were issued on compilations in the eighties. In *Ballads* and *Plays Duke Ellington* the sound quality is fine, but Webster sounds mostly routine. In the three tracks where Teddy Wilson sits down behind the piano he gets going a bit more, yielding a memorable version of "Stardust."[35]

A more interesting compilation is part of the series *Masters of Jazz*, with Danish studio work from 1968–'70. Ben plays more intensely here, and blew the ballad "Going Home," which had not been part of his discography until then.[36]

Live in Vienna contains a concert from May 2, 1972, with the Printers Jazzband, an amateur group consisting of Austrian printers and graphic artists. The music quality is a pleasant surprise: the supple mainstream septet is up there with Arnved Meyer's band. Webster's solos sound better than most records from this period. Unfortunately, the recording quality is substandard.[37]

Webster's final concert took place two weeks before his death in Leiden, the Netherlands. It was brought out on a two-LP set almost immediately. A gig with an uninspired rhythm section, a noisy audience and an old, sick soloist—nobody would have dreamed of issuing the record had it not been Webster's final performance.[38]

notes

1 *Live! Providence, Rhode Island*, Storyville.
2 *Stormy Weather*, Black Lion.
3 *The Jeep Is Jumping*, Black Lion.
4 *The Holland Sessions*, Blue Note.
5 *Coleman Hawkins Encounters Ben Webster*, Verve.
6 *Americans in Europe*, Fontana.
7 *Ben Webster in Europe, vol. 2*, Rarities 55 (LP).
8 *King of the Tenors*, Verve MGV 8020 (LP).
9 See note 2. "Danny Boy" is called "Londonderry Air" here.
10 *The Holland Sessions*, Blue Note.
11 *The New Grove Dictionary of Jazz* (Macmillan Press).
12 *Gone With the Wind*, Black Lion, and *Stormy Weather*, Black Lion. The music of the three original records is now available on two CDs.
13 *Ben Webster in Europe*, Rarities 45 (LP). The pieces are "Pennies From Heaven," "Blues in B," "My Romance," "In a Mellow Tone," "How Long Has This Been Going On," and "52nd Street Theme."
14 *There Is No Greater Love*, Black Lion, and *The Jeep Is*

Jumping, Black Lion.

15 *Hines' Tune*, Esoldun-Ina.

16 *With Steen Vig's Jazz Orchestra*, Storyville.

17 Duke Ellington/Ella Fitzgerald: *Ella & Duke at the Côte d'Azur*, Verve.

18 *Ben Webster in London*, Mercury/Fontana.

19 *Ben Webster Meets Bill Coleman*, Black Lion, and Various Artists: *Americans in Europe*, Fontana.

20 Henk Romijn Meijer, *Een Blauwe Golf aan de Kust* (Meulenhoff 1986).

21 *Ben Webster Meets Don Byas*, MPS.

22 *Ben Webster in Europe*, Rarities 55 (LP). The numbers are "You'd Be So Nice To Come Home To" and "I Got Rhythm."

23 *At Ease*, Ember CJS 822 (LP). Also on: *The Holland Sessions*, Blue Note.

24 *He Played It That Way*, IAJRC 30 (LP).

25 *For the Guv'nor*, Affinity.

26 *I Remember*, RCA/Black Elephant 822005 (LP).

27 *Gentle Ben*, Ensayo.

28 *My Man*, Steeplechase.

29 *Live in Paris*, Esoldun-Ina.

30 *Ben Webster's Dictionary*, Philips 6308101 (LP).

31 *Autumn Leaves*, Futura Swing (LP), and *Gentle Ben*, Ensayo ENY 3433 (CD).

32 *Live at the Haarlemse Jazzclub*, Cat, and *In Hot House*, Hot House.

33 *No Fool, No Fun*, Spotlite. The music of *Blow Ben, Blow* has been incorporated in the CD version of *For the Guv'nor*, Affinity.

34 *Ben Webster in Europe*, Rarities 45 (LP), the numbers "Perdido" and "Stardust."

35 *Plays Ballads*, Storyville, and *Plays Duke Ellington*, Storyville.

36 *Masters of Jazz*, Storyville.

37 *Live in Vienna*, RST 91529. Can be ordered from Rudolf Staeger, Schönbrunnerstrasse 14, A-1050, Vienna, Austria.

38 *Last Concert*, Bovema 5C178.24 964/5 (two-LP set). Also on: *The Holland Sessions*, Blue Note.

"...and i'm old and going"

Rob Agerbeek: "I remember one of the last times I played with him. That was in Orpheus, in Apeldoorn. With Tony Inzalaco and Henk Haverhoek. Ben stopped after just three numbers, and we had a break. But sooner or later we had to resume, so someone advised me to play a few trio pieces and let Ben come back on later. He wasn't drunk—just old. Old and tired. He gave me an impression of, 'Oh no, do I have to go out there again? I would rather have stayed in bed.' We were really working hard just to get through the evening.

"That concert was in May or June of 1973. I remember this clearly, because on the way home, I almost got hit by a train. I had taken a wrong turn, and suddenly found myself right before the railway tracks with a train on the way and not enough room to brake. I just managed to speed across the tracks, and was shaking like a leaf as the train thundered past right behind me.

"That was because I was so exhausted after that performance. I was absolutely beat. Because the evening had turned out so differently from what I had expected. Ben

was nowhere, and I had to fill all his gaps with trio pieces. And the bass player knew some pieces but not others... I just kept on playing—"All The Things You Are" and "I'll Remember April" and "I Let a Song Go out of My Heart," and so on. And after all that, we had to pull Ben out of the swamp again."

Jesper Thilo remembers: "He knew that he was getting old. He would say these short, telling phrases: 'Thilo, never get old, never get old.' I didn't see him as an old man. He was only just over sixty, but he felt old."[1]

Bent Kauling: "In Denmark, he changed his attitude towards a lot of things in the world. What he saw on

Danish and Swedish television made him very strongly against the American involvement in Vietnam. He called Nixon some funny names, sometimes. He wanted to become a Danish citizen and he could have been one in 1974, because by that time he would have lived permanently in Denmark for five years. But unfortunately he went to Holland and we never saw him again."[2]

When Jimmy Rowles spent a week with him in early 1973, he went on an old-fashioned bender. However, after Rowles' departure he tried to turn over a new leaf. He went to a doctor, began taking vitamin pills, and made sure he ate well.

His cousin Harley Robinson, who was working in Munich that year and visited his uncle every two weeks, recalled it was high time Ben started looking after his health. "The last time I saw him in Copenhagen, he was in a wheelchair! He was moving around in his little apartment that way. I was shocked, and asked him, 'What's the matter, man?' He said, 'I'm not feeling well, I'm too tired to walk.' "

Ben had been on the wagon for about three weeks when Birgit Nordtorp said goodbye to him at the Copenhagen train station, on September 2, 1973. He had to go on the road again because Wigt had planned a series of concerts in the Netherlands and Germany. This tour included a concert in the Dutch city of Leiden on September 6, and one in Cologne the very next day. On September 6, Ben spent the daytime attending Steven Kwint's exhibition with Johan van der Keuken, Rens

Sevinga, and Kwint himself. Later that day, the group went over to De Twee Spieghels, the establishment in Leiden where the concert was to take place.

Irv Rochlin was going to accompany him that night, with Inzalaco and Haverhoek. Rochlin: "Tony Inzalaco was living in Cologne, and as we were going to play there the next day, he thought it would be much smarter to just stay there. He could spend that day doing studio gigs until seven-thirty or so. That's why he asked Peter Ypma to substitute for him in Holland.

"When Ben entered De Twee Spieghels, he saw Peter busy setting up. He immediately asked gruffly, 'Where's Tony?' He didn't expect an answer; it was one of his now-frequent rhetorical questions. I started telling him what was going on, but he wouldn't listen. 'Tony's crazy,' he snarled. I said, 'Don't get mad, man, I can explain everything,' but he turned around and sat down at the bar in a terrible mood.

"Ben had nothing against Peter, but he had expected Tony, and it bothered him that things turned out differently. It threw him off right from the start. He ordered a brandy. The bartender gave him a glass of Dutch cognac. He took one sip and called, 'Hey man, what is this shit?' To which the bartender replied, 'That's Dutch brandy.' Ben wanted to say he would have preferred a French cognac, but was afraid that that would sound like an insult. So he stuck to Dutch brandy. The concert was terrible."

Henk Haverhoek: "He was mixing all kinds of drinks,

started drinking Scotch besides the cheap brandy, and so on. That didn't do him any good."[3] Johan van der Keuken: "He was getting agitated because the audience was quite noisy. It was a bunch of college students, frat rats who had no clue what was going on. They were yelling things just for the fun of it."

Rens Kwint: "The students' noisy chatter annoyed me tremendously. Ben was very emotional, tears were running down his cheeks. It was very distressing, I almost got a sore throat. I thought, 'Can't you shut up for just a moment? That man is opening himself up completely, and you noisy brats are oblivious.' Ben must have felt that this was the last night he could bring himself to perform."

The concert ended with Thelonious Monk's blues "Straight, No Chaser," and in spite of his exhaustion, Ypma's stiff playing, and the shameless chatter around him, Ben tried to turn it into a worthy finale. He blew his old licks one last time, haltingly and almost out of breath. It ended in a drum solo, after which Ben was incapable of repeating the theme once again. Instead, he started talking to the audience—something he seldom did. Haverhoek, "We all felt something was about to happen." He may have been trying to get the students to listen after all.

Slowly, in a clear voice, he said, "When I was just a little boy, an old man said to me, 'Son, you're young and growing and I'm old and going. So have your fun while you can.' " He repeated the last two sentences. The people in the audience, who had no clue what he meant to say, were quiet and embarrassed for a moment. Scattered applause followed.

On the record, the short speech seems appropriate, but van der Keuken looks back on it with sadness. "I remember the speech as something completely aimless and confused. He was completely isolated, facing an audience that didn't grasp the deeper meaning of his words at all. It was tragic."

After the concert, the group returned to Amsterdam in Steven Kwint's BMW. The weather was bad, and Van der Keuken describes the trip as a long, harsh journey. "Ben was probably drunk, but I later realized that something may already have been wrong with his brain at the time. We were driving around in a fog, literally and figuratively, and I noticed that Ben didn't know if he was in Holland, in Denmark or the United Sates. There was fog around us, wherever we looked, and the atmosphere was sad."[4]

Webster was dropped off at hotel De Haas near the Amsterdam Vondelpark, and helped up to his room. The next morning, around eleven, Rens and Steven paid him a visit. Webster needed regular Vitamin B injections because of his ravaged liver, and when he was in Amsterdam, Rens—who was a nurse by profession—would do this for him. She was shocked at how they found him in bed.

"He'd had a stroke that night. One foot hung over the edge of the bed, and the phone was off the hook. He must have tried calling someone. He managed to mumble a few words, which were very hard to make out. He was mumbling something about 'Betsy,' his saxophone. He had wet his bed—understandable, because he could hardly move—and I had some clean sheets brought up.

"It was a Saturday, and it took a whole morning's pleading to get him admitted somewhere. I called countless doctors and hospitals. I felt terrible—the man was gravely ill, yet nobody could find the time to help him. While I was busy arranging his care, Steven left to call off that day's concert. He took Ben's sax with him. I got mad at the doctor who finally arrived, because he took just one glance at Ben and started writing a bill."

The doctor called an ambulance, and at approximately 2 PM Webster was admitted to the Lucas Hospital in the west of the city. Nobody seemed to know him. Rens was assumed to be his wife, because she was taking care of his affairs. The doctors examined him, and soon diagnosed him with brain thrombosis. He lost consciousness that day and didn't regain it until Monday night. At a subsequent examination, on Tuesday, the doctors found he was partially paralyzed.

He was visited by Birgit Nordtorp and Billy Moore who had come over from Copenhagen, Inzalaco from Cologne, and his Dutch friends. In the course of his first week in the hospital he got a little better and became a bit more coherent. Wigt told the press that Ben was seriously ill, but that his condition was no longer critical.

Verspoor: "One side was paralyzed, so he could only speak a few syllables at a time. He did recognize us, addressed all visitors by name. His memory was still intact. He knew he would never be able to play the saxophone again. If he had survived, he'd have ended up in a wheelchair. But he kept this natural dignity."

After a week, he contracted pneumonia. According to Rens Kwint, something like that was to be expected. "The man was so unhealthy, he couldn't breathe very deeply and his liver was barely functioning at all. When your body is in such bad shape such things can happen. You simply don't have any resistance left."

The illness proved fatal. On the morning of September 20, 1973, Michiel de Ruyter got a phone call from the hospital: Ben was doing very badly, and the nursing staff hadn't been able to reach Steven and Rens. De Ruyter hurried to the hospital but right before he arrived, at eleven-thirty, Webster had passed away.

The deceased was laid out in the hospital for a couple of days, so that friends and family could take a last look, then transferred to Copenhagen. Two family members soon contacted his European friends. Ben's second cousin Joyce Cockrell sent a friendly letter to Steven and Rens from L.A. to tell them a few things about his youth, and to thank the two for all they had done for him.

Ben's cousin Harley—then an energetic, youthful 54-year-old insurance agent and tax adviser—came over to Copenhagen. He immediately decided that Ben ought to be cremated in Copenhagen; he thought that would be the practical and economical thing to do. Rens and Steven disagreed. They thought he would have wanted to be buried in Kansas City. He was attached to K.C., and would have objected to cremation on religious grounds. Steven was so upset about this that he stayed in the Netherlands. According to Rens, "He felt he had already said goodbye in Amsterdam."

Ben Webster's ashes were brought to the Assistens Kirkegaard in Copenhagen, a very old, renowned cemetery near the city center, where Søren Kierkegaard and Hans Christian Andersen were also buried.

At the church service in Copenhagen, Kenny Drew played the organ. One of the things he played was "All Too Soon," one of Ben's successes from the Ellington years. Milt Hinton, who had stayed in contact via telephone until shortly before Webster's death, sent his condolences by mail.

Reverend Johannes Møllehave gave a speech. "Ben Webster—I can see him now with his hat tilted back with the baggy skin beneath his eyes as puffed as his cheeks, his eyes closed, and the funny leak of breath often oozing out beside Betsy's mouthpiece, joining the conversation. I see him as the image of an oppressed people. A people to whom the freedom of expression in any other ways than music, songs, drums, horns, has not been granted... Imagine such a man transforming his fortunes into expressions more perfect than those of any language."[5]

Ben's gravesite, Assistens Kirkegaard, Copenhagen

※

Irv Rochlin and his then wife were among the people in the church, and he was deeply moved. His grief turned to anger when he got a call a few weeks later from someone at record company Bovema, who had gotten their hands on two cassettes that contained the last concert in De Twee Spieghels. A fan had taped the evening with two microphones. "I was unpleasantly surprised, because I had no idea that the evening had been recorded. I said, 'You shouldn't issue those, Ben didn't play well at all.' But the guy replied, 'I'm not calling to ask your permission. I just want to know the names of the pieces.' "[6]

※

In Holland, it took years before Ben Webster was awarded a lasting monument. In the eighties, however, a street was named after him in the neighborhood of Zevenkamp in Rotterdam. The Ben Websterstraat is a short, angular street, with the appropriate cross streets of Fats Wallerstraat and Art Tatumstraat. The Coleman Hawkinspad and Duke Ellingtonstraat are a short distance away. Webster would have been delighted with this token of appreciation.

notes

1 From the movie *The Brute and the Beautiful* by John Jeremy (1989).
2 See note 1.
3 See note 1.
4 See note 1.
5 The speech is quoted in these words on the cover of the

album *Ben Webster & Sweets Edison*, Columbia KG 327774 (two-LP set).

6 *Last Concert*, Bovema 5C178.24 964/5 (two-LP set). Also on: *The Holland Sessions*, Blue Note.

ol' betsy

Steff, you take care of Ol' Betsy and let nobody play her," Webster had said to Steven Kwint in the hospital. He was gravely ill, but the words came out clearly. Webster had bought Ol' Betsy, his antique tenor saxophone, in 1938. He had played it continually ever since; when the keys stopped working or the pads gave out, he would take it to a repair shop for a complete overhaul.

He visited the Selmer factory in Paris once where he, as a famous musician, was given a brand new tenor saxophone—along with an alto sax and clarinet—for next to nothing. But he stayed attached to Ol' Betsy. The new instruments were much lighter and made playing fast passages a lot easier, but they could not produce his deep, trademark sound. His new tenor, stained pink, usually stayed inside its case, and after his death went to Dexter Gordon, who played it for a few years.

Webster sometimes took up the clarinet at home when he hadn't played for a few days and wanted to work on his embouchure. To make things more challenging, he played it with a wide G mouthpiece, and a huge inflex-

ible reed. But otherwise, Ol' Betsy was his only instrument. The metal mouthpiece was an Otto Link number 8; the reed a three-and-a-half Rico V-style. Ol' Betsy herself was an ancient Selmer, of the "Balanced Action" type, serial number 25418. It had been built in 1938, and went through a few owners within that same year before Webster took possession of it.

※

Right after Ben's cremation, Harley Robinson went in search of his will. He inspected his apartment in Copenhagen, and demanded that the Kwints search the sax case once more, and that they ask Mrs. Hartlooper if she had any of his paperwork. The search yielded nothing even remotely resembling a will.

Robinson then wrote to them that they would just have to write to the curator—Bertil Jacobi, who we'll get to in a moment—to arrange for the return of the paintings Steven had loaned to Ben. The new saxophone, which had barely been played, was sold to Gordon—everyone agreed that that was an appropriate fate—but there was some confusion about the rest of his estate.

According to Bertil Jacobi, "We had a big problem. The deceased had left no testament, he was not married and had no children. He did have a cousin, but cousins aren't considered heirs under Danish law. In such cases, the estate usually goes to the State. We wanted his possessions to be used differently. We knew Ben Webster loved Denmark and its jazz scene. We knew we would be acting in his spirit if we donated the royalties from his records to Danish jazz. That is why we started

opposite: with Ol' Betsy, in concert, 1971

the Ben Webster Foundation, after consultation with the Ministry of Justice."

The foundation was acknowledged by the Danish queen on September 23, 1976, and is doing well. Foundation secretary Bertil Jacobi reported in 1999 that the foundation's annual income varies between 150,000 and 200,000 crowns, which is approximately 20,000 to 26,000 dollars. This money goes toward the annual Ben Webster award—generally awarded to young Danish musicians—and an annual Ben Webster party. Benny Carter and Harley Robinson are honorary members.

Meanwhile, Ol' Betsy was still at Kwint's house. Steven had placed the saxophone on top of his piano, in its open case. Visitors were allowed to look at the instrument, but—true to his word—he never let anyone play her. Nobody seemed about to claim it, until Ben's Danish acquaintance Billy Moore contacted Kwint.

On September 27, 1975, Moore wrote "Mrs. & Mr. Steffan Kwint" a cordial letter that ended on a businesslike note. In his opinion, the foundation ought to own the sax and grant aspiring jazz musicians an opportunity to use it. He instructed Steven to send Ol' Betsy to Copenhagen as soon as possible. Two weeks later, Steven sent him a letter in which he politely but firmly stated why he refused to hand over the instrument: Ben had asked him to take care of the saxophone on his deathbed, and until a suitable American museum was found, he would continue to keep and protect it. Ben's remarks in the hospital were legally binding, as witnesses had been present.

A heated correspondence between Moore and Kwint followed. Moore just would not be persuaded, even though honorary Foundation member Harley Robinson took the Kwints' side. "I trust you completely, and I don't see why Billy Moore has to poke his nose in everything," Harley wrote to Steven and Rens. Birgit Nordtorp was of the same opinion.

On September 18, 1977, almost exactly four years after his best friend passed away, Steven Kwint unexpectedly died of a cerebral hemorrhage while on vacation in France. He was only 45 years old. His wife subsequently washed her hands of the whole affair.

Michiel de Ruyter: "She asked me, 'Can't you take care of that saxophone?' And that's how Ol' Betsy came to stay with me for a while. Billy Moore wanted to have that sax to let young musicians play it. Which was nonsense—young musicians had no use for it. Willem Breuker visited me once and wanted to have a look at the thing. I said, 'Now watch it. You can take it out of its case, but don't play it.' Willem examined the sax and concluded, 'Modern musicians wouldn't be able to play the thing anyway.' It was such an old-fashioned saxophone, terribly heavy, and extremely heavy to play as well.

"I happened to be in the States in 1978, and there's a jazz museum there: the Institute of Jazz Studies at Rutgers University, New Jersey. Dan Morgenstern is the director. They have one of Kid Ory's hats there, and some of Billie Holiday's jewelry, Lester Young's sax, and all kinds of wind instruments that used to belong to

Roland Kirk. So why not Ol' Betsy?"

On February 17, 1979, de Ruyter wrote a letter to "Dear Dan," offering the tenor to the museum on a permanent loan basis. Ten days later, he received two letters back from Morgenstern. One was an official statement of acceptance. He promised that he would take good care of Betsy, and that no one would be permitted to play her. The second letter was more informal, "As you say, it's good that Ol' Betsy will be kept alongside the horn on which Prez made his recordings with Basie and Billie. This pair will be the jewels in our collection of memorabilia."

The sax is displayed there now, next to Young's, as promised, and in its original case. Jesper Thilo turned out to have the case, and after a phone call from de Ruyter, he sent it to Morgenstern without delay. De Ruyter didn't need to worry about transportation. A friend of his, Jaap Lüdecke, was a part-time radio worker, amateur sax player, and airline purser, which entailed monthly trips to New York. Lüdeke, "In early March, 1979, I went to pick up Ol' Betsy at Michiel's place. The instrument was at my house for a few days before I had to make the flight. Chiel had told me I wasn't allowed to play it, but he hadn't forbidden me to take a peek inside the case. In a compartment, I found two sax straps: an old one and a new one. I called Chiel and said, 'You know, I'm not letting it go just like that!' We talked about it, and he allowed me to keep the new one. I'm still using it for my alto.

"Then I was off. I put Ol' Betsy in the Boeing 747 safe.

That night I was at a hotel in Queens, and called Dan Morgenstern with the reassuring words, 'I'm here, and so is the saxophone.' We arranged to meet outside, on the corner of Broadway and 47th Street. So at nine the next morning, I took the subway.

"Exactly at the agreed time, Morgenstern was waiting there. It all went quite quickly; he had a busy day that day. That's why the transaction took place outside—there was no time for a leisurely chat in a café. Without much ceremony, he thanked me for my trouble, and left for the Institute in Newark right away." After this transfer, correspondence ended: nobody could argue with Ol' Betsy's final resting-place.

select discography

A list of "Ben Webster's most important records"—sent to me by Webster buff Joop Spuyman—contained some five hundred items. Many of them present the same music under different titles. In this chapter, I will concentrate on Webster's essential work, that is: records on which he is heard on more than just a few tracks, where his playing adds something to the rest of his oeuvre, or which are of historical interest for other reasons. The records are rated from one star—horrible—to five—indispensable. All records are CDs and issued under Ben's name, except where noted.

1 - Blanche Calloway: The Essential Blanche Calloway (Le Jazz/Charly Records) 1925–1935
**

A CD devoted to this vaudeville (and sometimes blues) singer, containing Ben's earliest solo efforts. He sounds like a real amateur. These recordings can also be found on *The Chronical Classics CD* (Classics).

2 - Bennie Moten: Bennie Moten's Kansas City Orches-

tra (Classics) 1930–1932
***1/2
Webster sounding more professional in a fine band that would later be led by Count Basie. Also on: *Basie Beginnings* (RCA).

3 – Fletcher Henderson: And His Orchestra (Classics) 1932–1934
***1/2
Ben making rapid progress as a young Coleman Hawkins fan in a band that is noted for its flashy ensemble playing. Also issued as *Tidal Wave* (GRP).

4 – Billie Holiday: The Quintessential Billie Holiday, Vol 1 (Columbia) 1933–1935
***1/2
5 – as above, Vol 2, 1936
****
6 – as above, Vol 3, 1936–1937
****
Holiday and Ben—her one-time lover—are getting better and better, as do their pick-up groups. Of course, no one could support her as well as Lester Young; he can be heard on vol. 3.

7 – Cab Calloway: Cab Calloway (Classics) 1934–1937
***
This one is dominated by Cab's extroverted singing, while his well-paid sidemen have to hold back. There are a few notable glimpses of Webster, though.

8 – Benny Carter: Benny Carter (Classics) 1933–1936
***1/2

Compilation of sessions under Carter's leadership, with Ben on a few tracks. He plays his first mature ballad solo on record here, "Dream Lullaby."

9 – Willie Bryant: Willie Bryant (Classics) 1935–1936
***1/2
Another compilation, this time with forgotten singer Bryant. Ben—present in two sessions—is excellent on "The Voice of Old Man River."

10 – Duke Ellington: Duke Ellington (Classics) 1935–1936
***1/2
Ben's first recordings with the Duke, as well as his first recorded solo in his band: "Truckin'." Not bad. Look for his second solo—"In A Jam"—on Duke Ellington, 1936–1937 (Classics).

11 – Teddy Wilson: Teddy Wilson (Classics) 1939
***
In the studio, Wilson's short-lived big band doesn't live up to its potential. Webster is fine, though, on "Some Other Spring."

12 – Teddy Wilson: Broadcasts (Fanfare) 1939
***1/2
The sound is mediocre, but the band plays with more fire on this live recording. Vinyl only.

13 – Duke Ellington: The Blanton–Webster Band (Bluebird) 1940–1942
*****
Just like Holiday's work with Webster, these recordings

have been reissued over and over again in various compilations. The best choice is this 3-CD set, with wonderful studio sessions of the Ellington band during Blanton and Webster's stay. A high point in the careers of everyone involved. More or less the same music can be found on a series of Classics discs.

14 – Various Artists: The Great Ellington Units (Bluebird) 1940–1941

****1/2

Some of the same musicians, now in small groups, and almost as good. The leaders are Johnny Hodges (the only one who didn't hire Ben), Rex Stewart, and Barney Bigard.

15 – Duke Ellington: Live From The Crystal Ballroom in Fargo, N.D., Vol. 1 (Tax) 1940

****

16 – as above, Vol. 2

****

It was a cold night, but the band sounds inspired and the new tenor player gets plenty of room. Also available as a double CD on Vintage Jazz Classics and Jazz Heritage.

17 – Duke Ellington: The Carnegie Hall Concerts (Prestige) 1943

****

Double CD with Ellington's band playing the "Black, Brown and Beige Suite" and other work. Four stars for the whole thing, although Ben is only sporadically featured.

18 – A Tribute to a Great Jazzman (Archives of jazz) 1936–1945

***

A compilation of live recordings, from Ellington to the John Kirby Sextet. Recording quality is so-so, the playing fine.

19 – James P. Johnson: James P. Johnson (Classics) 1943–1944

***

Studio sessions with solid accompaniment, led by one of Ben's favorite stride pianists.

20 – Coleman Hawkins: Rainbow Mist (Delmark) 1944

***1/2

Three fine studio sessions with Hawk, including an interesting meeting with Ben and a third tenor player, Georgie Auld.

21 – The Horn (Progressive) 1944

***

Small combo swing with trumpeter Hot Lips Page. Well done, but there are too many false starts and alternate takes on this issue. Also on Bluenite BN.

22 – Sid Catlett: Sid Catlett (Classics) 1944–1946

***

Various tracks, including six of Catlett's strong quartet with Ben, Marlowe Morris, and John Simmons.

23 – Walter 'Foots' Thomas: The Walter 'Foots' Thomas All Stars (Prestige/Bellaphon) 1944

***

Ben recorded with alto player Thomas on a couple of occasions, playing the blues—which was no problem at all for this tenor man from KC.

24 – Slim Gaillard: Laughin' in Rhythm (Verve) 1946–1954

***

Nutty sounds from hipster and comedian Gaillard, featuring Ben in a (probably) 1952 session. Highly enjoyable.

25 – The Complete Ben Webster on EmArcy (EmArcy) 1951–1953

***1/2

Various studio sessions, including both jazz gigs and a curious session with the vocal quartet The Ravens. Ben could have done far more gigs like this, if only he hadn't demanded 'triple scale.'

26 – Charlie Parker: Jam Session (Verve) 1952

***1/2

Norman Granz recorded Ben's most important work of the fifties. This (too polite) jam session was Ben's first recording with Granz, and featured, among others, Benny Carter, Johnny Hodges, Parker—and Webster, of course.

27 – Modern Jazz Quartet/Ben Webster: Live (Jazz Anthology) 1953

****

In concert with the recently founded MJQ, with Kenny Clarke still behind the drums. Ben sounds strong with this ideal rhythm section.

28 – King of the Tenors (Verve) 1953
****

With Oscar Peterson's quartet and—on some tunes—contributions from Benny Carter. Impeccable.

29 – Various Artists: JATP in Tokyo (Pablo) 1953
***

Lots of noise and shouting brass, but also some pretty ballads. Typical JATP stuff, with Ben doing "Someone to Watch over Me" and "Cotton Tail."

30 – Music for Loving (Verve) 1953–1955
***

The albums *Music with Feeling* and *Music for Loving*, together on a 2-CD set, with a Harry Carney date as a bonus. Well done, although Webster doesn't need strings; he is mellow enough on his own.

31 – Illinois Jacquet: The Kid and The Brute (Verve) 1953–1954
***1/2
Ben happened to be in the studio where Jacquet was recording with his seven-piece band. They put two lengthy blues pieces on tape. The rest of this CD is filled with jukebox stuff from Jacquet.

32 – Billie Holiday: All or Nothing at All (Verve) 1956–1957
****

Studio recordings with lavish accompaniment from Webster, brought together on this 2-CD set.

33 – Billie Holiday: Songs for Distingué Lovers (Verve) 1956
***1/2
A single CD featuring Ben again, as well as Harry Edison and Jimmy Rowles.

34 – Billie Holiday: The Complete Billie Holiday on Verve (Verve) 1945–1959
****
Box with ten CDs and a book, with everything Lady Day recorded for Norman Granz; includes some excellent 1956 and '57 sessions with Ben.

35 – Ben Webster–Art Tatum Quartet (Verve) 1956
***
Somewhat overrated encounter with Mr. Busy Fingers.

36 – Ella Fitzgerald: Sings the Duke Ellington Song Book (Verve) 1956–1957
****
Three-CD set with Ellington's band and a small group, featuring Ben Webster. Ellington was in a hurry, but the result is almost as good as could be.

37 – The Soul of Ben Webster (Verve) 1957–1958
***1/2
Two CDs with the music of three LPs: Ben's *The Soul of Ben Webster*, Johnny Hodges' *Blues A Plenty* and Harry Edison's *Gee Baby, Ain't I Good to You*. Ben's own session is fine; the others tend to be formulaic and repetitive.

38 – Benny Carter: Jazz Giant (Contemporary) 1957
***1/2

Easy swing by a great group. But this is probably of more interest to Carter fans—he shines on both the alto sax and trumpet—than for most readers of this book.

39 – Bill Harris: Bill Harris and Friends (Fantasy/ Milestone) 1957

****

Great meeting with Harris, a trombone player who can render a ballad as subtly and intimately as Webster.

40 – Soulville (Verve) 1957

*****

Unmissable session with Ben and Peterson's quartet, both at their most intense and most relaxed at the same time.

41 – Ben Webster/Coleman Hawkins: Encounters (Verve) 1957

****1/2

Recorded the next day, with Hawkins sitting in, and another well-chosen repertoire of mellow standards. Close to perfect.

42 – Billie Holiday: Broadcast Performances, vol. 3 (ESP) 1957

***

Airshots of uneven quality, but including the lengthy blues "Fine and Mellow" that Billie sang with Lester Young, Hawkins, Ben and other stars. From the touching TV special *The Sound of Jazz.*

43 – Michel Legrand: Legrand Jazz (Philips) 1957

****

Big orchestra, playing Legrand's arrangements, with a star-studded cast including Miles Davis and John Coltrane. Ben shines in "Nuages."

44–46 – Johnny Hodges: Side by Side (Verve) 1958
Not so Dukish (Verve) 1958
The Smooth One (Verve) 1959

***

Ducal companies, playing a lot of blues in an unspectacular but elegant way. Rather formulaic, but Ben always gets a chance to contribute a ballad or two.

47 – At The Nuway Club (Jazz Guild/Phontastic) 1958
***

Gig with a local band in Long Island. The sound is bearable, the band works hard and Ben seems to enjoy himself. Vinyl only.

48 – Ben Webster and Associates (Verve) 1959
***1/2
Nice meeting with tenor men Budd Johnson and Hawkins on some blues, and a long, long "In A Mellow Tone."

49 – Jimmy Witherspoon: The Spoon Concerts (Fantasy) 1959
***1/2
Spoon on stage, singing with renewed self-confidence. Strong support from Webster, Hawkins, and Roy Eldridge.

50 – Gerry Mulligan: Gerry Mulligan Meets Ben Webster (Verve) 1959
****

51 – The Complete Gerry Mulligan Meets Ben Webster (Verve) 1959
***1/2

Number 51 is a double CD with the complete session (of the series 'Mulligan Meets'), showing that these two could get along fine. 50 is a single CD with the highlights only.

52 – Ben Webster Meets Oscar Peterson (Verve) 1959
*****

Another classic with Peterson, including faultless, touching performances of "The Touch of Your Lips" and "In the Wee Small Hours of the Morning."

53 – Ultimate Ben Webster (Verve) 1954–1959
****

54 – Quiet Now/Until Tonight (Verve) same period
***1/2

Two attractive compilations. *Ultimate* was curated by young tenor man James Carter, who picked a mixed background (from The Ravens to Peterson), the latter features too many strings.

55 – Jo Stafford: Jo + Jazz (Corinthian) 1960
***1/2

Jo Stafford loved jazz and could sing jazz. To demonstrate that, she made this recording, supported by Ellingtonians including Ray Nance, Johnny Hodges, and Webster.

56 – Helen Humes: Song I Like to Sing (Contemporary) 1960
****

Singer Humes with a small big band playing modern Marty Paich arrangements, and a combo featuring Webster. Perhaps her best work ever.

57 – At the Renaissance (Contemporary) 1960
***1/2
Webster in his favorite club with a great band that includes Jimmy Rowles. The sound could have been better and Webster's solos longer.

58 – The Warm Moods (Discovery) 1961
***
Hard-to-get stuff with strings he doesn't really need. Originally on Sinatra's Reprise label.

59 – Richard Groove Holmes: With Ben Webster (Pacific Jazz) 1961
***1/2
Organ player Mr Groove was a big man with a huge sound and a lot of blues feeling. Subtlety was not his strong point, but Ben knows how to handle a gig like this.

60 – Benny Carter: BBB&Co (Original Jazz Classics) 1962
**1/2
The three B's are Benny, Ben, and Barney Bigard. Which means that this could have been a great record, if only the guys didn't sound as if they were struggling with a bad hangover.

61 – Frank Sinatra: And The Swingin' Brass (Reprise) 1962

***

Ben doesn't get a lot of space, but the collaboration of The Brute and a cheerful Ol' Blue Eyes alone secures the record a place in this overview.

62–63 – Jimmy Witherspoon: & Ben Webster (Reprise) 1962; Live (Stateside) 1962
***

The blues again, with Spoon and Ben. Pretty much more of the same.

64 – Ben & Sweets (Columbia) 1962
***1/2
Ben's "My Romance" sounds close to definitive. Sweets Edison, to quote a critic, "noodles alongside in his happiest lazybones matter."

65 – Clark Terry: More (Cameo) 1963
***1/2
Despite the title, this is definitely not just more of the same. A capable sextet, on a vinyl record that is hard to get.

66 – Soulmates (Original Jazz Classics) 1963
***1/2
The other soulmate is Joe Zawinul, his young friend and roommate, who does a fine job on the acoustic keyboard. Thad Jones sits in on cornet.

67 – Ben Webster/Gene Ammons: Tenor Giants (Enja) 1964
***

Routine gig with Junior Mance, which is combined with

another run-of-the-mill gig of Gene Ammons on this CD.

68 – See You at The Fair (Impulse) 1964
****

Fine studio dates with Hank Jones and Roger Kellaway alternating at the piano. Includes a memorable "Over the Rainbow."

69 – Clark Terry: The Happy Horns of Clark Terry (Impulse) 1964
***1/2

Like Terry's 'More', you will have to look hard for this one too. Solid studio date with a sextet, playing mainly Ellington material.

70 – Milt Hinton: Here Swings The Judge (Famous Door) 1964
**1/2

Vinyl only. Diverse material, including three tracks from Hinton's basement with Ben talking, blowing, and trying to play the piano.

71 – Live! Providence, Rhode Island (Storyville) 1964
**1/2

The recording is done by an amateur, and the trio isn't up to Ben's standards, but his playing is not bad.

72 – Lionel Hampton: You Better Know It!!! (Impulse) 1964
***1/2

Lightweight but entertaining studio date with Hampton and a first-rate NY rhythm section.

73 – Oliver Nelson: More Blues and The Abstract Truth

(Impulse) 1964
***1/2
Ben's last studio gig in the USA: a guest spot on three tracks with Nelson, an arranger who tried to give the traditional blues a 'new' sound.

74–76 – Stormy Weather (Black Lion) 1965
Gone with The Wind (Black Lion) 1965
There Is No Greater Love (Black Lion) 1965
****
In a couple of marathon sessions with what would soon become his favorite European rhythm section (Kenny Drew, piano, young Niels-Henning Ørsted-Pedersen, bass, Alex Riel, drums), Ben recorded enough material for some wonderful albums. Also issued by Jazz Life.

77 – The Jeep Is Jumping (Black Lion) 1965
***1/2
Same time, same town (Copenhagen) and almost the same high level. Ben with the trumpeter Arnved Meyer's Ellington-like band.

78 – Duke Ellington: At Juan-Les-Pins (Verve) 1966
****
79 – Duke Ellington and Ella Fitzgerald: Côte d'Azur Concerts (Verve) 1966
***1/2
Ben sitting in on a couple of songs with Ellington's band and Ella Fitzgerald, trying to ignore Ray Nance, who was over-refreshed. 79 is an 8-CD set with all the music Ellington and Ella recorded there, including five tunes with Ben.

80 - Ben Webster in London (Mercury/Fontana) 1967
***1/2
Good tenor playing, although piano player Dick Katz is a little over-industrious, and organ player Allen Haven (who appears on only three tracks) is downright boring. Also issued—as *Big Ben Time!*—by Philips.

81 - Americans in Europe (Fontana) 1967
**1/2
Studio session with tenor men Eddie Miller, Eddie Lockjaw Davis, and Bud Freeman. Could have been great if there had been a stimulating rhythm section. Vinyl only.

82 - Meets Bill Coleman (Black Lion) 1967
**1/2
Another try with this rhythm section, this time with trumpeter Bill Coleman. Not much better.

83 - Ben and Buck (Storyville/Sackville) 1967
***
Concert in Belgium. Ben and Buck Clayton could have been a fine team, but they don't play together much and the recording sound quality leaves something to be desired.

84–86 - Plays Duke Ellington (Storyville) 1967–1971
Plays Ballads (Storyville) 1967–1971
Master of Jazz (Storyville) 1968–1970
***1/2
Nice compilations of mostly Danish radio recordings. Reasonable sound, hard-working bands varying from the Drew/NHØP/Riel unit to the Danish Radio Big Band,

featuring Ben at his most laid back.

87 – Meets Don Byas (MPS) 1968
* *
Strangely uninspired meeting, with Webster playing too little and Byas too much.

88 – The Holland Sessions (Blue Note) 1969–1973
*/**/***
Three LPs on two CDs. One star for *At Ease* (with the amateur trio of Frans Wieringa), which should have stayed in the files. Two for *Last Concert*, which might have stayed there as well. Only three for *For The Guv'nor*, where Cees Slinger plays great but Ben sounds strangely distant.

89 – For The Guv'nor (Affinity) 1969
/*
Two LPs brought together on one CD. Two stars for a weird date with Kenny Drew, and Wieringa on piano (initially issued as *Blow, Ben, Blow*), and three again for *For The Guv'nor*.

90 – Live in Amsterdam (Affinity) 1969
***
A club date with Cees Slinger and his men once again, with Ben sounding more energetic, but this time the piano is hardly audible.

91 – Ben op Zijn Best (Westside) 1970
****
The best Webster record you never heard. This collection of gospels and folk songs with a fine Dutch septet

was reissued shortly afterwards as *I Remember Ben* on RCA, and then completely forgotten. Vinyl only.

92 – No Fool, No Fun (Spotlite) 1970
**1/2
Hilarious rehearsal with the Danish Radio Big Band. Completists only.

93 – Wayfaring Webster (Daybreak/Challenge) 1970
***

Radio date with Slinger, with Ben sounding pretty energetic.

94 – Live in Vienna (RST Records) 1972
***

Concert with a semi-pro Austrian band. Much better than you may fear, but hard to get.

95–96 – Live at the Haarlemse Jazzclub (Cat) 1972
Ben Webster in Hot House (Hot House) 1972
**1/2
Club dates in Holland with Tete Montoliu. The band is so-so and Ben seems to be lacking energy.

97 – Live in Paris (Esoldun/Ina) 1972
***

French radio concert, with a better sound and Ben sounding really serious on "Old Folks." It would have been nice if the sidemen's solos had been shorter.

98 – Gentle Ben (Ensayo) 1972
***

Ben's last recording date in a studio, this time—for a change—in Spain. Not bad, although the trio lacks fire.

99 – Ben Webster Dexter Gordon Baden (TCOB) 1972
***1/2
Good playing from Kenny Drew and especially Gordon, but unfortunately the two tenors hardly play together; they simply do their own features.

100 – My Man (SteepleChase)
**1/2
Ben's last planned record date, at the Montmartre Jazz Club. He feels old and tired, and that, unfortunately, is how he sounds.

index of names